250 ESSENTIAL KANJI
FOR EVERYDAY USE

VOLUME TWO

250
ESSENTIAL KANJI
FOR EVERYDAY USE

生活の中の漢字

VOLUME TWO

KANJI TEXT RESEARCH GROUP
UNIVERSITY OF TOKYO

TUTTLE PUBLISHING
Boston • Rutland, Vermont • Tokyo

Published by Tuttle Publishing,
an imprint of Periplus Editions (HK) Ltd.,
with editorial offices at 153 Milk Street, Boston, Massachusetts 02109.

LCC Card No. 97-81452
ISBN 0-8048-3638-8

First edition, 1998

Printed in Singapore

Distributed by:

Japan
Tuttle Publishing
Yaekari Building, 3rd Floor
5-4-12 Osaki, Shinagawa-ku
Tokyo 141-0032
Tel: (03) 5437 0171; Fax: (03) 5437 0755
Email: tuttle-sales@gol.com

North America, Latin America & Europe
Tuttle Publishing
Airport Industrial Park
364 Innovation Drive
North Clarendon, VT 05759-9436
Tel: (802) 773 8930; Fax: (802) 773 6993
Email: info@tuttlepublishing.com
www.tuttlepublishing.com

Asia Pacific
Berkeley Books Pte. Ltd.
130 Joo Seng Road, #06-01/03
Singapore 368357
Tel: (65) 6280 1330; Fax: (65) 6280 6290
Email: inquiries@periplus.com.sg

05 07 08 06 04
3 5 7 8 6 4 2 1

To the Learners

Welcome to ESSENTIAL KANJI FOR EVERYDAY USE, Volume Two. How do you feel about studying kanji? These exotic and alien characters are all around you as you go about your daily life in Japan, and at first they may seem impossible to learn. Well, they're not. If you start by becoming familiar with kanji encountered on a daily basis, you'll feel much more comfortable in Japan. You'll no longer have to walk down the street oblivious to written warnings, no longer miss out on sales because you couldn't read the advertisements, and no longer be in social and cultural limbo because of an inability to read entertainment listings.

ESSENTIAL KANJI FOR EVERYDAY USE, Volume One, which introduces the first 250 kanji, was published in 1993. Volume Two will teach you another 250 kanji that most frequently appear in daily life. Each of the following 22 lessons illustrates situations in places you are likely to find yourself in Japan, dealing with personal computers, electric appliances, highways, and supermarkets. All the tools you need to feel comfortable and to accomplish your goals in these environments are right here in this book.

Each lesson is divided into an exercise section and a kanji section. The quizzes found in the exercise section will help you learn the kanji characters and kanji compounds that relate to the situations presented in the text. In the kanji chart, memory aids have been included to help you understand and remember the kanji. The compounds introduced are made up with the acquired kanji to help you understand the new words clearly and quickly.

After completing your study of the kanji in this textbook, you should feel quite at home in a variety of everyday situations. We sincerely hope that this will make your life in Japan both easier and more enjoyable.

Junko Ishida
Akiyo Nishino
Yoshiko Yamazaki

Kanji Text Research Group
Japanese Language Class
Department of Civil Engineering
Graduate School of Engineering
University of Tokyo

はじめに

本書の目的と特徴

　本書は1993年7月にチャールズ・イー・タトル出版社から出版された ESSENTIAL KANJI FOR EVERYDAY USE の続編であり、主に非漢字圏の日本語学習者が日常生活に役立つ漢字を生活の場面を通して、Volume One と Volume Two を合わせて 500 字学ぶ初歩の教科書である。また、サバイバルの漢字で終わらないように、より進んだ漢字学習へとつなげることも目指している。そして、何よりも、興味を持って楽しく学べることが本書のねらいである。

　来日当初から駅での表示や交通標識、銀行や郵便局等の窓口、あるいは店や食堂、その他の施設で使われている漢字を目にし、意味が理解できずに困ることが多い。このように日常よく目にする漢字の意味が分かれば、日本での生活が容易になる。生活に役立つ漢字を覚えれば、繰り返しその漢字に接触するので、学習した漢字が無理なく定着する。そして、その後の漢字学習に対して意欲が持てるようになる。Volume Two では更に多くの場面を設定し、そこに現れる漢字を課題を通して学習できるように工夫した。提示した漢字は実際に目にする表記を重んじた。

　漢字チャートの熟語は、なるべく既習の漢字と組み合わせるようにした。熟語を学習することによって、一つの漢字がほかの漢字と結びついて新しい熟語を構成していくという漢字の造語力に気付かせ、応用力を身に付けることを期待した。また、漢字の成り立ちの説明や覚え方のヒントを与えて、漢字の形と意味の関連を示し、学習者が興味を持って漢字を学ぶことができるように配慮した。

本書作成の背景

　本書は、もともと東京大学大学院工学系研究科社会基盤工学専攻の留学生のために、初級漢字教育の教科書として作成されたものである。社会基盤工学専攻では、1982 年 10 月から留学生に対して日英二か国語を使用言語とし、日本語でも英語でも学位が取れる態勢を整えた。従って、学生は英語で専門教育が受けられるので、学業のための日本語は必要としない。しかし、大学内外での生活をより円滑にするために、社会基盤工学専攻独自で日本語教育を行っている。漢字教育もその一部である。

　はじめは、日本語の教科書に沿って漢字を教えていたが、上記の日本語教育の目的に添うように、新たに、学生の身のまわりにある言葉を場面ごとに分類した "KANJI AND KATAKANA AROUND YOU" を作った。その中から必要度が高いと思われる 500 の漢字を選んで、"EASY WAY TO KANJI" を 1988 年 5 月に作成し、漢字教科書として使った。1989 年度には文部省から教育方法等改善費が与えられたので、それを機会に改めて 250 の漢字を選択し、タイトルを「生活の中の漢字」として内容も豊富に作り替えた。そして、"250 ESSENTIAL KANJI FOR EVERYDAY USE"として、1993 年にタトル社から出版されたわけである。この Volume One に引き続き、今回 Volume Two を出版するに当たって、さらに、当教室の学生だけではなく、生活のために漢字の学習を必要としている一般の学習者にも役立つように心がけた。

作成過程

　東京大学社会基盤工学専攻の日本語教室の学生（留学生、研究員、教官とその配偶者）を対象に、漢字を必要とする場面についてインタビューやアンケート調査を行った。その結果に基づいて、いろいろな場所へ学生と一緒に出かけて行き、生活に必要な漢字の写真を撮った。

　これらの写真に加えて、銀行での手続きや定期券購入などに必要な用紙、食堂のメニュー、大学の諸手続きの用紙類、学生の意見や彼らが生活の中でメモをした漢字リスト、留学生の世話を

している日本人学生に対するアンケート調査などを資料として、場面別の漢字熟語リストを作った。Volume Two では、仕事で日本に滞在している外国人や、その家族などからも意見を求め、学生というより、一般の外国人が日本で生活する上で必要と思われる場面と 250 の漢字を選んだ。漢字の選定に当たっては、必要度の高い漢字、資料の中でよく使われていた漢字、そして、その漢字の造語力なども考慮した。

　各場面は、イラストや実物、写真などで構成し、その場面で遭遇するであろう問題に対して適切な行動がとれるような課題をつけた。

本書の構成と使い方

　本書は 22 課から成る。各課は、1. Introductory Quiz（場面と質問）、2. Vocabulary（語彙表）、3. New Characters（新出漢字）、4. Practice（練習問題）、5. Supplement（補足）から構成されている。各課の最初の頁にその課で扱われている場面や写真や実物および簡単な説明をつけた。そして、巻末には付録、解答、音訓索引、語彙索引をつけた。1.と 4.と 5.には、未習の漢字と、"ESSENTIAL KANJI FOR EVERYDAY USE" Volume One, Volume Two の漢字以外のものにはふりがなを付けた。2.と 3.では、"ESSENTIAL KANJI FOR EVERYDAY USE" に取り上げられていない漢字には×印を付けた。なお、ローマ字の表記はヘボン式を使用した。

各課の構成と使い方は、以下のとおりである。

1. INTRODUCTORY QUIZ（場面と質問）

　日常生活で出会う場面のイラストとクイズからなる。まず、2.の語彙表を参照しながら、イラストの中にあることばの意味を知る。次にクイズに答えることにより提示された場面の内容を理解する。ここでは、学習者が実生活で遭遇するであろう場面を目にすることによって学習意欲が湧き、場面に結びつけて漢字やことばの意味を理解する事を目的とする。漢字を学習した後でもう一度語彙表を見ずにやってみることをすすめる。教室では実生活での経験を交えて日頃の疑問点などを話し合うのも効果的であろう。

2. VOCABULARY（語彙表）

　場面と質問で使われていることばの読み方と意味が載せてある。イラストの理解や、質問に答えるときに参照してほしい。漢字の上の数字はその漢字を学習する課を示す。×印の漢字は 500 字に含まれていない。

3. NEW CHARACTERS（新出漢字）

　新出漢字のリストと漢字チャートからなる。チャートには新出漢字の意味、基本的な音訓読み、書き順、成り立ちや覚え方のヒント、熟語とその英訳が載せてある。熟語欄には、原則として新出漢字と既習漢字との組み合わせによってできたことばを上段に載せた。下段にある熟語には、500 字に含まれない漢字との組み合わせもあるが、余裕のある学生はぜひ参考にしてもらいたい。送りがなは慣用的なものを優先した。

4. PRACTICE（練習問題）

　まとめとして、漢字の読み書きを練習する。出題の対象となっていることばは、3.の熟語欄の上段のもので、下段のものは扱っていない。解答はついていないので、チャートで確認してほしい。

5. SUPPLEMENT（補足）

　課によって、その課に関連することばや写真や用紙類を載せた。

本書の出版に当たって、多くの方々にお世話になった。イラストは、前回と同様に東京大学の卒業生で、現在宇都宮大学工学部建設学科池田裕一氏が引き受けてくださった。筆順も、前回と同様に社会基盤工学専攻の秘書の関口京子氏にお願いした。同専攻日本語教室日本語講師仲間には、この漢字の本を作り始めた時からいろいろな面で支援してもらった。マイクロソフト・オフィス 97 での版下作りには、社会基盤工学専攻に関係する多くの人々に助けられた。

　また、この本を世に出してくださったチャールズ・イー・タトル社、編集部内のスタッフ及びウインストン・プリースト氏に深く感謝申し上げる。
　漢字の成り立ちに関しては学習研究社刊「漢字源」を主に参考にさせていただいた。
　次の方々には、写真や資料などを快く提供していただいた。心からお礼を申し上げたい。（50 音図表順、敬称は省略させていただく。）

株式会社イトーヨーカ堂	鶴見国際交流の会
江崎グリコ株式会社	東京都文京区役所
江戸東京博物館	日本道路公団
後楽園遊園地	富士サファリパーク
住宅都市整備公団	松下電器産業株式会社
財団法人そごう美術館	宮田雅之アートプロモーション株式会社雅房

　この本を教科書や自習用テキストとして使っていただき、率直なご批評やご感想をいただければ幸いである。

東京大学大学院工学系研究科
社会基盤工学専攻日本語教室
漢字教材研究グループ

石　田　順　子
西　野　章　代
山　崎　佳　子

Contents

THE LESSONS

Lesson	Subjects Covered	Kanji Introduced	Page
1 アパートをかります Information from Real Estate Agents and Magazines	Rental housing	家 賃 管 理 戸 建 共 交 利 当 良 好 向 活	21
2 公団住宅に申し込みます How to Apply for Public Housing	Application for public housing	公 宅 居 募 集 在 身 元	31
3 新東京国際空港 Procedures and Facilities of the New Tokyo International Airport	Airport	港 旅 客 免 税 両 替 続 待 合 荷 関 到	39
4 外国人登録を変更します Application for a Change of Alien Registration	Alteration of registered items	役 変 更 登 録 請 姓 職 父 母	49
5 きょうはなにが安いですか Shopping at a Supermarket	Supermarkets	額 価 得 乳 冷 凍 塩 直 送 枚 組	57
6 ちかくの店で買います Strolling Along a Shopping Street	Shops at a mall or on a shopping street	写 真 具 花 米 酒 古 美 容 焼 軽	65
7 ゴミの出し方 Putting Out the Garbage	Types of garbage and recycling	器 積 収 可 燃 粗 制 類 願 指 以 缶	73
8 ともだちの家へ行きます Visiting Friends	Reading maps	私 石 町 駐 川 校 育 園 示 村 転 現	81
9 この食品の材料はなんですか How to Read Food Labels	Food labels	原 材 植 油 脂 調 味 賞 限 製 存 要 蔵 添 加	89
REVIEW EXERCISE	Lessons 1–9		98
10 どの洗剤を使いますか Cleansers for the Kitchen and Clothing	Household cleansers	衣 台 剤 庭 質 綿 毛 白 野 菜 果	99
11 ルーム・エアコンの使い方 How to Use a Room-Temperature Remote Control	Air conditioning	暖 房 運 温 設 風 強 弱 度 量	107
12 ビデオの使い方 Using a VCR	VCR functions	説 次 音 声 多 重 再 画 源 早	115

CONTENTS

Lesson	Subjects Covered	Kanji Introduced	Page
13 パソコンを使いましょう Using a Personal Computer	Computer words	漢 英 編 規 削 除 印 刷 換 選 検 了	123
14 旅行します Reading Travel Brochures	Traveling	泊 宿 往 復 海 幹 朝 昼 夕 由	133
15 温泉に行きます Sightseeing Buses and Hot-Spring Baths	Tourist attractions	観 光 寺 神 婦 殿 浴 泉	141
REVIEW EXERCISE	Lessons 10–15		148
16 車を運転します Driving on the Expressways	Signs on the highways	路 優 輪 徐 点 型 落 渋 滞 流 走	149
17 天気予報 How to Read Weather Forecasts	All about the weather	天 報 夏 冬 晴 雨 曇 雪 力 数 字 側 最 低 圧	157
18 年賀状を書きましょう Sending Cards	Cards and letters	賀 状 広 島 県 結 婚 招 返 信 御 欠 配 達 求 窓	167
19 デパートで買い物をします Shopping at a Department Store	Department stores	形 供 服 催 決 算 総 化 粧 段	179
20 めいしを交換します Exchanging Name Cards	Job titles	課 係 長 青 社 作 林 員 秋 春 夫 助 授	187
21 休みの日はなにをしますか What to Do on the Weekend	Entertainment options	術 楽 映 体 遊 般 臨	197
REVIEW EXERCISE	Lessons 16–21		204
22 文化講座に申し込みます Applying for a Culture Course	Application by postcard	座 参 初 心 持 締 効 満 問 希 望	205

Appendixes

Introduction

This book contains 22 lessons introducing 250 additional kanji. Each lesson focuses on an everyday situation that you may encounter in Japan. Before Lesson 1, there is a brief introduction of kanji and kana, and after every several lessons there are review exercises. The *On-Kun* Index and the Vocabulary Index are found at the end. This book is designed as a textbook for you to use both in the classroom and while studying on your own.

Organization of the Lessons

Each lesson is divided into the following sections.

The chapter title pages present pictures and cultural notes that give you a brief introduction to each lesson. Hiragana is given alongside kanji that you have not yet learned or are not included in the basic 500 kanji. A modified Hepburn system of romanization has been used.

1 INTRODUCTORY QUIZ

This section illustrates situations that you may encounter in daily life, and is followed by a quiz. By referring first to the words in VOCABULARY, you will learn the readings and the meanings of the words introduced in the lesson. Taking the quiz will lead you to an understanding of the situation presented in the illustration, and trying the quiz again after studying each kanji is a good review technique.

2 VOCABULARY

This section contains the readings and meanings of the words used in the INTRODUCTORY QUIZ, and you should refer to it when studying the illustrations or taking the quiz. The numeral above each kanji indicates the lesson where the kanji is introduced.

3 NEW CHARACTERS

This section introduces new kanji and their meanings, along with basic *on-kun* readings, stroke orders, etymologies or memory-aid hints, and compounds with their English translations. The compounds essentially consist of newly or previously introduced kanji. Kanji that are not included in the 500 taught in the two parts are marked with ×. More important compounds are shown in the upper part of the list. However, you are encouraged to study those in the lower part of the list as well. When kana is optionally added to kanji *(okurigana),* the most common usage is adopted and formal usages are shown in parentheses.

4 PRACTICE

This section provides practice for reading and writing the kanji in the upper part of the kanji charts. You should use the practice as a final check for the kanji learned in each lesson. Answers to the practice problems are not provided in this textbook.

5 SUPPLEMENT

Some lessons contain related supplemental information, forms, and/or photographs.

Kanji

The oldest Chinese characters, the precursors of kanji, originated more than 3,000 years ago. Originally they were simple illustrations of objects and phenomena in everyday life, and developed as a writing tool mainly characterized by pictography and ideography. Thus each of the Chinese characters carries its own meaning within itself.

Chinese characters, or kanji, can be classified according to origin and structure into four categories:

    1. Pictographic characters are derived from the shapes of concrete objects.

                → 木 → 木 =   tree

                → ⊖ → 日 =   sun

    2. Sign characters are composed of points and lines that express abstract ideas.

       • →   → 上 =   above

       • →   → 下 =   below, down, under

    3. Ideographic characters are composed of combinations of other characters.

        木 (tree) ＋ 木 (tree) →   林 = woodland

        日 (sun) ＋ 月 (moon) →   明 = bright

    4. Phonetic-ideographic characters are composed of combinations of ideographic and phonetic elements. Upper parts or right-hand parts often indicate the reading of the kanji. About 90% of all kanji fall into this category.

        先 (セン previous)   →   洗 (セン wash)

        安 (アン peaceful)   →   案 (アン proposal)

The Japanese had no writing symbols until kanji were introduced from China in the 5th century. Soon after this, kanji were simplified into phonetic symbols known as hiragana and katakana. Thus the Japanese language came to be written in combinations of kanji and kana (see page 15).

This kanji-kana writing system is more effective than writing with kana only. As the written Japanese language doesn't leave spaces between words, kanji among kana make it easier for readers to distinguish units of meaning and to understand the context. Readers can easily grasp the rough meaning of written text by following kanji only.

Kanji can usually be read two ways. These readings are referred to as *on-yomi* and *kun-yomi*. *On-yomi* is the Japanese reading taken from the original Chinese pronunciation. *Kun-yomi* is the pronunciation of an original Japanese word applied to a kanji according to its meaning. Hiragana added after *kun-yomi* readings are called *okurigana*. *Okurigana* primarily indicates the inflectional ending of a kanji, though the last part of the stem is occasionally included in the *okurigana*.

Most kanji are composed of two or more elements, and parts of one kanji are often found in different compounds in other kanji. Certain commonly shared parts are called radicals, or *bushu* in Japanese. Radicals are used to classify kanji in dictionaries; thus each kanji is allocated only one radical. Each radical also carries a core meaning. For example, the radical 言 means "word" or "speak." Therefore the kanji 語 (language), 話 (speak, story), 読 (read), 記 (note down), and 論 (discuss) all have something to do with the meaning of 言. There are 214 radicals altogether. Some frequently seen radicals, other than the ones already introduced in Volume One, are listed below.

1. 冫 ice   2. 彳 step   3. 女 woman   4. 刂 knife   5. 广 slanting roof
6. 尸 corpse   7. 禾 grain   8. 糸 thread   9. 門 gate   10. 灬 fire

Kanji strokes are written in a fixed direction and order. There are several fundamental rules for writing the strokes.

1. horizontal strokes: from left to right

    三 (three)   土 (soil)   工 (engineering)

2. vertical or slanting strokes: from top to bottom

    十 (ten)   木 (tree)   人 (man)   八 (eight)

3. hook strokes: from top left to right or left bottom

    日 (day)   手 (hand)   分 (minute)   氏 (surname)

4. the center stroke first, followed by the left and right strokes

    小 (small)   山 (mountain)

5. the outside strokes first, followed by the middle strokes

    月 (moon)   中 (inside)

6. the horizontal stroke first, followed by the vertical stroke (usually followed by another horizontal stroke)

    十 (ten)   土 (soil)

7. the left-hand slanting stroke first, followed by the right-hand side

    八 (eight)   六 (six)

As your knowledge of kanji increases, kanji dictionaries become more helpful. There are three ways to refer to a kanji.

1. Look for the kanji by radical in the *bushu* (radical) index.
2. Look for the kanji by stroke number in the *kakusuu* (stroke number) index.
3. Look for the kanji by pronunciation in the *on-kun* reading index.

Kana

Japanese Writing Systems

There are four different kinds of characters used for writing Japanese: kanji, hiragana, katakana, and romaji (Roman alphabet). Kanji incorporates meaning as well as sounds. Hiragana, katakana, and romaji are phonetic characters that express only sounds. However, unlike English, one kana character can be pronounced only one way: 「あ」 or 「ア」 is only pronounced [a].

Japanese sentences are usually written with a combination of kanji, hiragana, and katakana. Katakana is mainly used for foreign words that are adapted to fit Japanese pronunciation. Kanji appears in nouns, verbs, adjectives, and adverbs. Hiragana is primarily used to show the inflectional endings of kanji *(okurigana)*. Particles, conjunctions, and interjections are mostly written in hiragana. Although hiragana can substitute for kanji, a combination of kanji and hiragana is much faster to read. For example:

私は毎朝早く起きます。出かける前にテレビを見ます。

わたしはまいあさはやくおきます。でかけるまえにテレビをみます。

Watashi-wa maiasa hayaku okimasu. Dekakeru mae-ni terebi-o mimasu.

I get up early every morning. I watch TV before I leave home.

hiragana ——— あ a
romaji ———
katakana ——— ア

Japanese Syllabary Chart

Each square □ represents one pronounced syllable.

	a	i	u	e	o
	あ a / ア	い i / イ	う u / ウ	え e / エ	お o / オ
k	か ka / カ	き ki / キ	く ku / ク	け ke / ケ	こ ko / コ
s	さ sa / サ	し shi / シ	す su / ス	せ se / セ	そ so / ソ
t	た ta / タ	ち chi / チ	つ tsu / ツ	て te / テ	と to / ト
n	な na / ナ	に ni / ニ	ぬ nu / ヌ	ね ne / ネ	の no / ノ
h	は ha / ハ	ひ hi / ヒ	ふ fu / フ	へ he / へ	ほ ho / ホ
m	ま ma / マ	み mi / ミ	む mu / ム	め me / メ	も mo / モ
y	や ya / ヤ		ゆ yu / ユ		よ yo / ヨ
r	ら ra / ラ	り ri / リ	る ru / ル	れ re / レ	ろ ro / ロ
w	わ wa / ワ				を o / ヲ

ya	yu	yo
きゃ kya / キャ	きゅ kyu / キュ	きょ kyo / キョ
しゃ sha / シャ	しゅ shu / シュ	しょ sho / ショ
ちゃ cha / チャ	ちゅ chu / チュ	ちょ cho / チャ
にゃ nya / ニャ	にゅ nyu / ニュ	にょ nyo / ニョ
ひゃ hya / ヒャ	ひゅ hyu / ヒュ	ひょ hyo / ヒョ
みゃ mya / ミャ	みゅ myu / ミュ	みょ myo / ミョ

りゃ rya / リャ	りゅ ryu / リュ	りょ ryo / リョ

ん n / ン

g	が ga ガ	ぎ gi ギ	ぐ gu グ	げ ge ゲ	ご go ゴ
z	ざ za ザ	じ ji ジ	ず zu ズ	ぜ ze ゼ	ぞ zo ゾ
d	だ da ダ	ぢ ji ヂ	づ zu ヅ	で de デ	ど do ド
b	ば ba バ	び bi ビ	ぶ bu ブ	べ be ベ	ぼ bo ボ
p	ぱ pa パ	ぴ pi ピ	ぷ pu プ	ぺ pe ペ	ぽ po ポ

ぎゃ gya ギャ	ぎゅ gyu ギュ	ぎょ gyo ギョ
じゃ ja ジャ	じゅ ju ジュ	じょ jo ジョ

びゃ bya ビャ	びゅ byu ビュ	びょ byo ビョ
ぴゃ pya ピャ	ぴゅ pyu ピュ	ぴょ pyo ピョ

Additional Katakana

Created with small ア イ ウ エ オ ュ

	a	i	u	e	o	yu
y				イェ ye		
w		ウィ wi		ウェ we	ウォ wo	
kw	クァ kwa	クィ kwi		クェ kwe	クォ kwo	
gw	グァ gwa	グィ gwi		グェ gwe	グォ gwo	
sh				シェ she		
j				ジェ je		
t		ティ ti	トゥ tu			デュ tyu
d		ディ di	ドゥ du			デュ dyu
ts	ツァ tsa	ツィ tsi		ツェ tse	ツォ tso	
f	ファ fa	フィ fi		フェ fe	フォ fo	フュ fyu
v	ヴァ va	ヴィ vi	ヴ vu	ヴェ ve	ヴォ vo	ヴュ vyu

Derivation of Kana

Hiragana and katakana are Japanese phonetic syllabaries developed from kanji in the 8th century. Hiragana, which are cursive letters, derive from the shapes of entire kanji characters. Katakana, which are combinations of straight lines, derive from various parts of kanji characters. In some cases both hiragana and katakana are derived from the same kanji, such as *ka, mo, te, yu, ra,* and *ri,* on the opposite page. Kana derived from some of the kanji introduced in this textbook are also shown.

i 以 ん ろ い

mi 美 み み

ka 加 か か
ka 加 か カ

yu 由 ゆ ゆ
yu 由 ゆ ユ

mo 毛 も も
mo 毛 も モ

ra 良 ら ら
ra 良 ら ラ

ta 多 る タ

ri 利 り り
ri 利 り リ

te 天 て て
te 天 天 テ

ru 流 流 ル

Sample Kanji Chart

A sample from the kanji charts is explained below.

① ② ③ ④

6 建	build た・てる、(だ・て)、ケン	フ フ ヨ ヨ ⦆ 聿 ⦆聿 ⦆建
		建

聿 is the pictograph of a brush held straight up, and ⻌ means to go forward. In ancient China, the architect drew a building plan and when he was finished, the laborers moved ahead to begin the construction.	建てる　　たてる　　　　to build 建物　　　たてもの　　　building …◇… 一戸建て　いっこだて　　house 二階建て　にかいだて　　two-story house 建設する　けんせつする　to construct

⑤ ⑥ ⑦

① The kanji and its serial number in this textbook.
② Meanings.
③ Readings: *kun*-readings in hiragana, and *on*-readings in katakana. Hiragana following a dot [・てる in the sample above] are *okurigana*. Readings in parentheses ( ) express euphonic change, i.e., modified readings [e.g., た・てる、(だ・て)]. Only the first level readings are listed here.
④ Stroke order.
⑤ Etymology or memory-aid. (The authors have created new derivations for some kanji when the etymology is unclear or confusing.)
⑥ Important compound words, and their readings and meanings.
⑦ Additional compound words, and their readings and meanings.

Note: 1) Kanji marked ˣ are not included in the 500 kanji taught in ESSENTIAL KANJI FOR EVERYDAY USE, Volume One and Volume Two.
2) Kana in parentheses ( ) in kanji compounds is optional when writing [e.g., 終 (わ)る can be written 終わる or 終る]. Two sets of ( ) appear for most nouns derived from compound verbs. The kana in both ( ) or in the former ( ) only may be omitted, but the kana in the latter ( ) alone cannot be omitted [e.g.,取(り) 消(し) can be written 取り消し、取消し、or 取消、but not 取り消].
3) * indicates exceptional readings.
4) Small numbers placed above certain kanji in the Vocabulary sections refer to Lesson numbers in this book.

THE LESSONS

アパートをかります

Information from Real Estate Agents and Magazines

ONE OF the most important decisions for foreigners moving to Japan is about housing. In searching for apartments or houses to rent, magazine and real estate agents' listings are the most helpful. Many weekly magazines are published to give the latest housing information, while local real estate agents hang apartment-for-rent notices in their office windows. There are various kinds of apartment floor plans, with studio and 1DK apartment layouts being the most common. Rental rates are usually highest in the city center and lower in the suburbs. In this lesson, you will learn several technical terms that will be of use to you when negotiating your lease.

1 ☐ INTRODUCTORY QUIZ

Look at the illustrations below and refer to the words in VOCABULARY. Then try the following quiz.

Mike Smith is going to rent an apartment or a house for his family, who will come to Japan to live for a few years. Compare the following two options. Which do you think is appropriate for the Smith family?

a ## みどりの中の生活

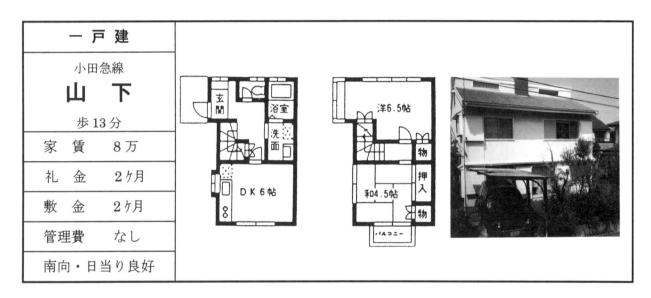

b ## 買物・交通便利なアパート

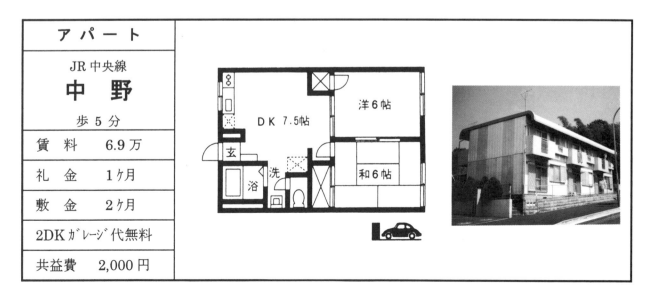

2 VOCABULARY

Study the readings and meanings of these words to help you understand the INTRODUCTORY QUIZ.

1.	賃料	ちん りょう	rent (apartment)
2.	家賃	や ちん	rent (house)
3.	管理費	かん り ひ	administrative fee
4.	礼金	れい きん	key money
5.	敷金	しき きん	deposit
6.	一戸建	いっ こ だて	house
7.	共益費	きょう えき ひ	maintenance fee
8.	便利な	べん り な	convenient
9.	木造	もく ぞう	wooden
10.	二階建	に かい だて	two-story (housing)
11.	無料	む りょう	free of charge
12.	南向き	みなみ むき	facing south
13.	日当たり	ひ あ たり	sunshine
14.	良好	りょう こう	good
15.	交通	こう つう	traffic
16.	生活	せい かつ	daily living

3 NEW CHARACTERS

Fourteen characters are introduced in this lesson. Use the explanations to help you understand and remember the characters. Study the compound words to increase your vocabulary.

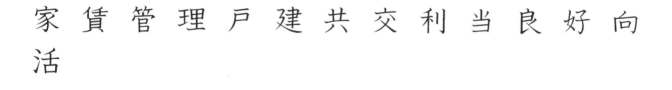

家 賃 管 理 戸 建 共 交 利 当 良 好 向
活

1 家

house, family

いえ、カ、ヤ

1	`	宀	宀	宀	宁	字	家
家	家						

Pigs 豕 were important animals in ancient China, and they were kept in the house 宀 where people lived. The original meaning is to roof animals like pigs, and it has changed to mean a building with a roof.

家	いえ	house
家内	かない	wife
大家	おおや	landlord/landlady
	… ◇ …	
画家	がか	painter, artist
作家	さっか	author

2 賃

fare, wages

チン

ノ	イ	㇑	任	仟	任	任	賃
賃	賃	賃	賃	賃			

任 is a combination of a person イ and the load 壬 the person is carrying, thus meaning responsibility. 任 combined with 貝＝賃, meaning the amount of money one is responsible for paying.

家賃	やちん	rent
電車賃	でんしゃちん	train fare
賃料	ちんりょう	rent
	… ◇ …	
賃金	ちんぎん	wages
賃貸	ちんたい	rented

3 管

pipe; control

カン

ノ	㇒	ケ	ケ	ㇰㇰ	ㇰㇰ	ㇰㇰ	ㇰㇰ
竹	竹	竺	管	管	管		

官 means round, and when a bamboo 竹 is added, 管 means a bamboo whistle with a circular cut tip.

入管	にゅうかん	immigration office
	… ◇ …	
水道管	すいどうかん	water pipe
気管	きかん	windpipe, trachea
鉄管	てっかん	iron tube

4 理	reason, logic, principle リ	一	丁	千	王	王	玑	珇	珇
		理	理	理					

The king, or ruler, 王 of the village 里 is reasonable.

管理	かんり	management
管理人	かんりにん	supervisor; superintendent
理学部	りがくぶ	faculty of science
	… ◇ …	
料理	りょうり	cooking
修理	しゅうり	repair

5 戸	door; house と、コ	一	ラ	ヨ	戸				

戸 depicts a door.

戸	と	door
	… ◇ …	
戸外	こがい	outdoors
戸数	こすう	number of houses

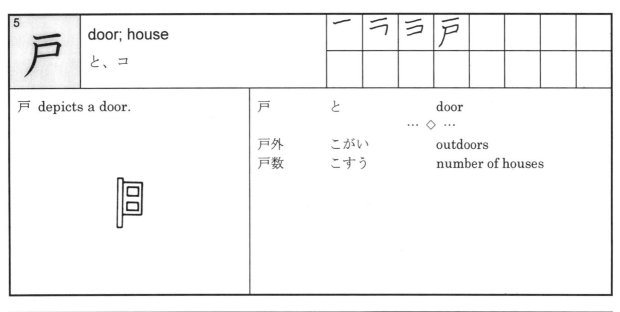

6 建	build た・てる、（だ・て）、ケン	ヿ	ヲ	ヨ	ヨ	彐	聿	津	建
		建							

聿 is the pictograph of a brush held straight up, and 廴 means to go forward. In ancient China, the architect drew a building plan and when he was finished, the laborers moved ahead to begin the construction.

建てる	たてる	to build
建物	たてもの	building
	… ◇ …	
一戸建て	いっこだて	house
二階建て	にかいだて	two-story house
建設する	けんせつする	to construct

7 共　together, both, all
とも、キョウ

一　ナ　サ　芏　芹　共

This is a pictograph of both hands together holding one thing.

共に	ともに	together
共益費	きょうえきひ	management fee
	… ◇ …	
共通の	きょうつうの	common
共同の	きょうどうの	cooperative
公共の	こうきょうの	public
男女共学	だんじょきょうがく	coeducation
共和国	きょうわこく	republic

8 交　intersection, coming and going, exchange
コウ

亠　一　亠　六　亦　交

Six 六 people are at work and interacting 乂. Thus 交 means to cross or exchange.

交通	こうつう	transportation
交番	こうばん	police box
	… ◇ …	
交代する	こうたいする	to take turns
交際する	こうさいする	to socialize
外交	がいこう	diplomacy
国交	こっこう	diplomatic relations

9 利　advantage; interest
リ

丿　仁　千　禾　禾　利　利

Grain 禾 and a plow リ combined, 利 means profitable, because if you plow the earth, you will reap more grain, which is a benefit to you.

便利な	べんりな	convenient
利用する	りようする	to use
利用者	りようしゃ	user
	… ◇ …	
有利な	ゆうりな	advantageous
不利な	ふりな	disadvantageous
利子	りし	interest (on a loan)

10 当	hit; on target あ・たる、トウ	丨	⺌	⺌	当	当	当		

Light ⺌, focusing (striking) on a hand ヨ.

当たる	あたる	to hit
日当たり	ひあたり	be sunny
本当の	ほんとうの	true
	… ◇ …	
当日	とうじつ	that day
当分	とうぶん	for the time being

11 良	good よ・い、リョウ	丶	㇕	㇉	𰀁	𫝀	良	良	

White 白 rice cooked over a fire 火 tastes good 良.

良い	よい	good
	… ◇ …	
良心	りょうしん	conscience
不良品	ふりょうひん	inferior goods

12 好	like す・き、コウ	く	女	女	女	好	好		

Women 女 like 好 children 子.

好き	すき	like
良好	りょうこう	good
	… ◇ …	
好物	こうぶつ	favorite food

13 向	face toward む・く、コウ	ノ	イ	竹	向	向	向		

The air flows out through the window 口 of a house in one direction.

南向き	みなみむき	facing south
方向	ほうこう	direction
	… ◇ …	
外人向け	がいじんむけ	for foreigners
向学心	こうがくしん	love of learning
向上心	こうじょうしん	desire to improve oneself

14 活	life; activity カツ、（カッ）	`	゛	シ	シ	シ	汁	汗	活
		活							

舌 is a pictograph of a tongue and water 氵, meaning wet tongue, thus 活 means life and, by extension, activity.

生活	せいかつ	living
	… ◇ …	
活発な	かっぱつな	lively
活用	かつよう	practical use
活動	かつどう	activity
活字	かつじ	print

4 PRACTICE

I. Write the readings of the following kanji in hiragana.

1. 家 賃   2. 管 理 人   3. 利 用 者   4. 共 益 費
                                                        えき

5. 良 好   6. 日本料理が、好きです。

7. 二階建ての家を建てます。

8. 戸を開けます。

9. これは、南向きの日当りが良い家です。

10. 本当に交通が便利です。

11. 理学部の建物は、どれですか。

12. 道が分からない時は、交番で聞いてください。

13. 日本の生活になれました。

Ⅱ. Fill in the blanks with appropriate kanji.

1. や ちん
rent

2. かん り
management

3. りょう こう
good

4. り
学部
faculty of science

5. こう
通
transportation

6. り
便 な
convenient

7. す
きです
to like

8. む
南 き
facing south

9. た
てる
to build

10. や
大
landlord

11. あ
たる
to hit

12. よ
い
good

13. かつ
生
living

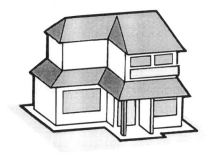

5 SUPPLEMENT

Rental Housing Contract

入居申込書					平成	年	月	日		
賃	フリガナ			生 年	年 月 日生			人員		
	氏 名			月 日						名
借	住 所			電 話						
	勤務先			電 話						
人	所 在			移 転						
	本 籍			理 由						
業務内容		役職		勤続年数	年	月収				

入	氏 名	年令	続柄	勤務先又は学校所在	電 話 番 号
居					
者					

連	氏 名		本人との続柄		年令	
帯	住 所					
保	勤務先					
証	所 在					
人						
業務内容		役 職	勤続年数		年	月収
住 居	持 家	一戸建	マンション	賃借物件	社 宅	借 家

物 件 名 称				
決 済 日	年 月 日	契 約 始 期	年 月 日
引 越 予 定	年 月 日	鍵引渡個数	個	印

賃借明細書	賃料 月分	日分日割		介手数料（消費税を含む
	賃料 月分			日受領仲介手数料(△)
	費 月分	日分日割		差 引 残 金
	費 月分			
	敷 金			
	礼 金			
	合 計			③ 諸 費 用 計
				（決済日に下記金額をご持参下さい）
	申 込 金 （△）			
	① 差引 残高			①＋②＋③合計 円
受付		契約書		残金受領		印鑑証明	有・無

This is a sample of a Japanese rental housing contract. Contract forms are not always identical, but this can serve as a reference. The contract used by realtors is written in Japanese. If there is any unclear point in the contract, you must clarify it before signing.

公団住宅に申し込みます

How to Apply for Public Housing

IN ADDITION to privately owned rental accommodations, there are rental apartments available in public housing projects, which are managed by local governments or public corporations. The public housing projects usually incorporate convenient facilities such as a shopping area, schools, post offices, banks, parks, and a community center. Within public housing projects, there are some rental apartments reserved for low-income families. Information about and applications for rental accommodations in public housing projects are available from the local city or ward office. After your application is accepted, as a foreigner you will be required to submit a certified copy of your foreigner registration documents. In this lesson, you will learn how to fill in a sample application form for public housing.

1 INTRODUCTORY QUIZ

Look at the illustration below and refer to the words in VOCABULARY. Then try the following quiz.

Mike prefers to rent accommodations in a public housing project because he need not pay a deposit, gift money, or commission to a real estate agent. Nor will he require a guarantor (身元保証人). Here is an application form for an apartment. Choose the number from 申込区分 and fill in the form following the example.

賃貸住宅空家入居者
空家募集のご案内
住宅・都市整備公団
住宅募集センター

申込区分	地区名	募集戸数	団　地　名	基準月収額（円以上）	団地一覧表頁（別売）	7年5月応募倍率
861－CD	み さ と 1	2	みさと	191,000	211	64.0
862－CD	み さ と 2	1	みさと	220,000	212	40.0
900－CD	取 手 井 野 1	2	取手井野	164,000	215	32.0

空家賃貸住宅入居申込書　平成　年　月募集

申込本人	住　所	横浜市北区中町10-5			
	TEL	(045) 000-0000			
	ふりがな 氏　名	マイク スミス	年令 26才	月収 20万円	
	明治・大正・昭和 43 年 7 月 27 日生(男・女)				
	勤務先 名称	ATC エンジニヤリング゛		落選回数	
	所在地	東京都 中央区 31-3		3	
	TEL	03-3812-2111 内線(6140)			

続柄	氏　名	年令	勤務先	月収
妻	メアリースミス	25		万円
子	トム スミス	1		

申込区分
861 ― CD

Courtesy of Housing and Urban Development Corporation.

2 VOCABULARY

Study the readings and meanings of these words to help you understand the INTRODUC-TORY QUIZ.

1.	賃貸住宅	ちん たい じゅう たく	rented accommodations
2.	空家	あき や	house for rent, space available
3.	入居	にゅう きょ	moving into (an apartment)
4.	募集	ぼ しゅう	application
5.	都市整備公団	と し せい び こう だん	Housing and Urban Development Corporation
6.	申込本人	もうし こみ ほん にん	applicant applying in person
7.	勤務先	きん む さき	one's place of work
8.	名称	めい しょう	name
9.	所在地	しょ ざい ち	address
10.	月収	げっ しゅう	monthly income
11.	同居	どう きょ	living with (someone)
12.	世帯員	せ たい いん	household member
13.	続柄	つづき がら	relationship
14.	地区名	ち く めい	name of the area
15.	戸数	こ すう	number of houses
16.	団地名	だん ち めい	apartment building name
17.	基準月収額	き じゅん げっ しゅう がく	required monthly income
18.	身元保証人	み もと ほ しょう にん	guarantor

3 NEW CHARACTERS

Eight characters are introduced in this lesson. Use the explanations to help you understand and remember the characters. Study the compound words to increase your vocabulary.

公 宅 居 募 集 在 身 元

15 公	public コウ	ノ	ハ	公	公			

Eight 八 and individuals ム combined, 公 means public.	公団	こうだん	public corporation
	公式	こうしき	official
	公立	こうりつ	public
		… ◇ …	
	公平な	こうへいな	fair
	不公平な	ふこうへいな	unfair

16 宅	house, home タク、（タッ）	'	'	宀	宀	宅	宅	

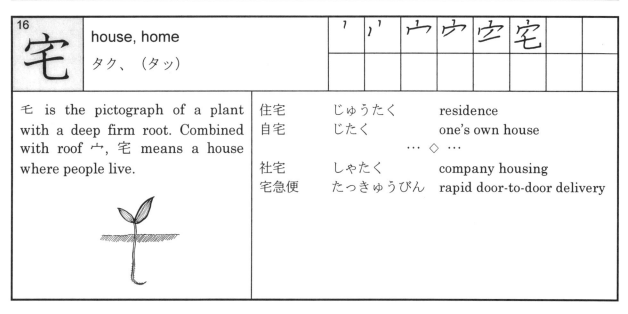

モ is the pictograph of a plant with a deep firm root. Combined with roof 宀, 宅 means a house where people live.	住宅	じゅうたく	residence
	自宅	じたく	one's own house
		… ◇ …	
	社宅	しゃたく	company housing
	宅急便	たっきゅうびん	rapid door-to-door delivery

17 居	exist, be い・る、キョ	コ	コ	尸	尸	尼	尼	居	居

To stay in a house 尸 for a long time and get old 古 combined, 居 means to stay.	居る	いる	to stay, to be
	入居者	にゅうきょしゃ	resident
	居間	いま	living room
		… ◇ …	

18 募	appeal for; invite application ボ	一	十	サ	艹	芍	芦	昔	苜
		茣	莫	募	募				

莫 literally means dark or, by extension, it means cannot be seen or does not exist. Hence combined with power 力, the kanji suggests there is not enough (man) power and it is necessary to recruit more.

募金	ぼきん		fund raising
		··· ◇ ···	
公募	こうぼ		offer for public subscription

19 集	gather あつ・まる、あつ・める、シュウ	ノ	イ	イ′	仁	什	伃	隹	隹
		隹	隼	隼	集				

Birds 隹 of a feather flock together (to a tree 木).

集まる	あつまる	to assemble
集める	あつめる	to collect
募集する	ぼしゅうする	to recruit
	··· ◇ ···	
特集	とくしゅう	special issue
集中する	しゅうちゅうする	to concentrate

20 在	exist; be located ザイ	一	ナ	才	右	存	在		

Water in a dam 才 with soil 土 remains still. Thus 在 means to be or to exist.

所在地	しょざいち	address
	··· ◇ ···	
現在	げんざい	at present
在日大使館	ざいにちたいしかん	embassy in Japan

21 身 み、シン	body	⁄	⁄	勺	勺	刍	身	身	

This is a pictograph resembling a pregnant woman. Thus it means to be filled with many things like muscles; a body.	身長	しんちょう	body height
		… ◇ …	
	出身地	しゅっしんち	hometown
	身分	みぶん	status
	中身	なかみ	contents

22 元 もと、ガン、ゲン	origin, foundation	一	二	テ	元				

儿 suggests body, emphasizing the legs, and 二 suggests the head. The head is thought to be the origin of human beings.	身元保証人	みもとほしょうにん	guarantor
	元気な	げんきな	vigorous
		… ◇ …	
	元日	がんじつ	New Year's Day
	三次元	さんじげん	three dimensions

4 PRACTICE

I . Write the readings of the following kanji in hiragana.

1. 公 団   2. 住 宅   3. 入 居 者   4. 募 集   5. 所 在 地

6. 身元保証人は、どなたですか。

7. 先生、お元気ですか。

8. 募金で、お金を集めます。

9. 身長は、160 センチです。

10. これが、自宅の電話番号です。

11. 切手を集めるのが、好きです。

II. Fill in the blanks with appropriate kanji.

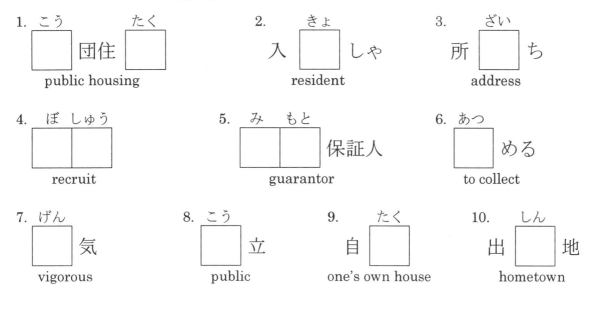

1. こう 〔 〕団住〔たく〕
public housing

2. 入〔きょ〕しゃ
resident

3. 所〔ざい〕ち
address

4. 〔ぼ〕〔しゅう〕
recruit

5. 〔み〕〔もと〕保証人
guarantor

6. 〔あつ〕める
to collect

7. 〔げん〕気
vigorous

8. 〔こう〕立
public

9. 自〔たく〕
one's own house

10. 出〔しん〕地
hometown

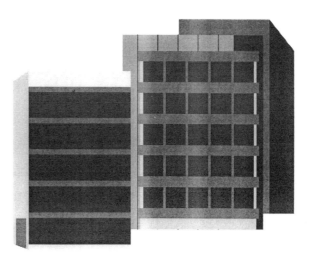

Portable Telephones　携帯電話

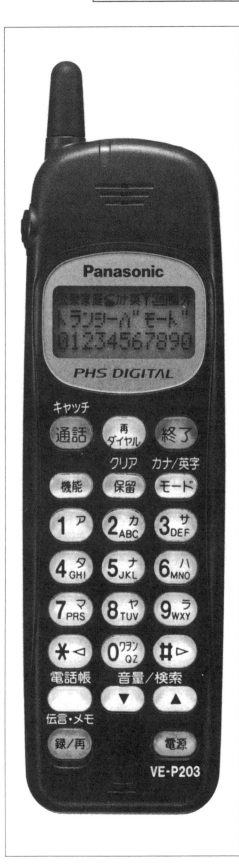

携帯電話 (けいたいでんわ)	portable telephone
通話 (つうわ)	call
再ダイヤル (さい)	redial
終了 (しゅうりょう)	off
機能 (きのう)	function
保留 (ほりゅう)	hold
モード	mode
カナ／英字 (えいじ)	kana/English
電話帳 (でんわちょう)	telephone directory
音量／検索 (おんりょう／けんさく)	volume/find
伝言・メモ (でんごん)	message/memo
録／再 (ろく／さい)	record/play
電源 (でんげん)	power

新東京国際空港

Procedures and Facilities of the New Tokyo International Airport

NEW TOKYO International Airport, or Narita, is one of the busiest airports in the world. Although you can get by using only English at the airport, it is a convenient place to learn kanji. There are many services available to help you get through the airport smoothly, and if you know kanji it is easier to take advantage of these services. For example, kanji can help you to plan the route and means of transportation to reach the airport. You can also take advantage of a service that will deliver your baggage directly to the airport, so you don't have to carry it yourself. And watch the signs, so that you don't forget to declare your valuables at the customs desk! In this lesson, you will learn terms for facilities at the airport.

1 INTRODUCTORY QUIZ

Look at the illustrations below and refer to the words in VOCABULARY. Then try the following quiz.

I. Mike is leaving Japan to meet his family in his home country. He has just arrived at the New Tokyo International Airport (Narita) Terminal 2. There are various facilities at the airport, as shown below. Fill in the spaces with the correct letters (a～f).

1. みやげものが、安くかえます。　　　　　　　　　　　　　　　　（　　　）
2. 日本のお金をほかの国のお金にかえます。　　　　　　　　　　（　　　）
3. 空港で分からないことがあったら、ここで聞きましょう。　　（　　　）
4. 日本を出国するために、手続きをします。　　　　　　　　　　（　　　）
5. ひこうきにのるまで、ここで待ちます。　　　　　　　　　　　（　　　）
6. ここは、第2旅客ターミナルです。　　　　　　　　　　　　　（　　　）

Ⅱ. Mike is returning to Japan with his family.　To enter Japan, follow the course below.

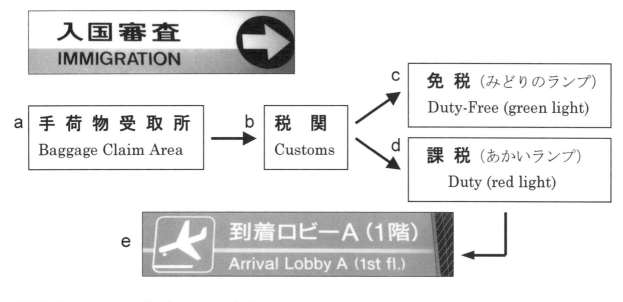

Fill in the spaces with the correct letters (a〜e).

1.　入国審査の後、（　　　　　）で、自分の荷物を受け取ります。

2.　そのつぎに、（　　　　　）へ行きます。

3.　税金をはらわないとき、（　　　　　）へ行きます。

4.　税金をはらうとき、（　　　　　）へ行きます。

5.　ともだちが、（　　　　　）で待っています。

2 VOCABULARY

Study the readings and the meanings of these words to help you understand the INTRODUC-TORY QUIZ

1.	空港	くう こう	airport
2.	新東京国際空港	しん とう きょう こく さい くう こう	New Tokyo International Airport
3.	旅客ターミナル	りょ きゃく ターミナル	airport terminal
4.	案内所	あん ない しょ	information
5.	空港公団	くう こう こう だん	Airport Authority
6.	免税売店	めん ぜい ばい てん	duty-free shop
7.	両替	りょう がえ	currency exchange
8.	出国手続	しゅっ こく て つづき	passport control/procedure for departure
9.	待合室	まち あい しつ	waiting lounge
10.	入国審査	にゅう こく しん さ	Immigration

11.	手荷物受取所	て に もつ うけ とり しょ	baggage claim area
12.	税関	ぜい かん	customs
13.	課税	か ぜい	duty
14.	免税	めん ぜい	duty-free
15.	到着ロビー	とう ちゃく ロビー	arrival lobby

3 NEW CHARACTERS

Thirteen characters are introduced in this lesson. Use the explanations to help you understand and remember the characters. Study the compound words to increase your vocabulary.

港 旅 客 免 税 両 替 続 待 合 荷 関 到

---

23 港	harbor, port みなと、コウ	ヽ シ シ シ 汁 汗 洪 洪	洪 洪 港 港

巷 is a pictograph of streets. 氵 means water. 港 thus refers to shipping lanes and a port.

港	みなと	harbor
空港	くうこう	airport
成田空港	なりたくうこう	Narita Airport

··· ◇ ···

| 港町 | みなとまち | port city |

巷

---

24 旅 — trip, travel / たび、リョ

` | ` 亠 | ` 方 | 方 | 方' | 扩 | 扩 | 旅
旅' | 旅

旅 is the pictograph of a flag flying in the wind. 衣 suggests that two men are walking in a row under the flag like travelers in a caravan. It means journey.

| 旅 | たび | trip |
| 旅行 | りょこう | trip |

··· ◇ ···

旅券	りょけん	passport
旅費	りょひ	travel expenses
旅館	りょかん	Japanese-style inn

25 客 — guest, customer / キャク

` | ` ' | 宀 | 宀 | 宀' | 安 | 安 | 客
客

Someone who stops 各 at a house 宀 is a guest 客.

| 旅客 | りょきゃく | traveler |
| お客様 | おきゃくさま | guest, customer |

··· ◇ ···

| 客間 | きゃくま | guest room |

26 免 — escape; exempt / メン

ノ | ク | 夕 | 夕 | 岛 | 岛 | 免 | 免

A man ク with two big mouths 口 and long legs ル is a strong man who can run away from an enemy. Thus 免 means to escape.

| 免税 | めんぜい | duty-free |

··· ◇ ···

| 免税店 | めんぜいてん | duty-free shop |
| 免税品 | めんぜいひん | tax-free goods |

27 税	tax ゼイ	ノ	ニ	千	耂	耒	禾	禾゛	秒
		秒	稻	秒	税				

Government 兄 or big brother with two horns ソ on the head collects grain 禾 as taxes.	税金	ぜいきん	tax
		… ◇ …	
	住民税	じゅうみんぜい	residence tax
	無税	むぜい	tax free

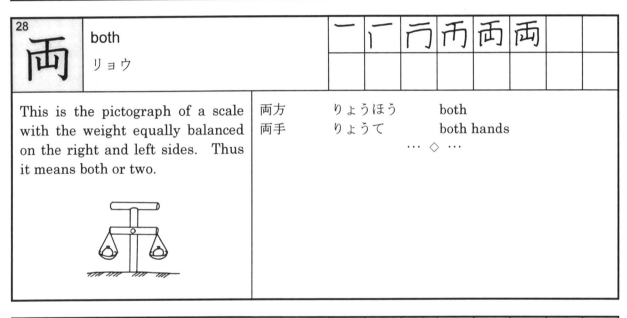

28 両	both リョウ	一	丆	亓	丙	両	両		

This is the pictograph of a scale with the weight equally balanced on the right and left sides. Thus it means both or two.	両方	りょうほう	both
	両手	りょうて	both hands
		… ◇ …	

29 替	replace, substitute; exchange か・える、（が・える）	一	二	亖	夫	夫゛	夫二	耂夫	夫夫
		夫夫	替	替	替				

It is an accepted norm that two men cannot spend the day 日 sharing one office. One has to be replaced, substituted, or exchanged by the other.	替える	かえる	to replace
	両替する	りょうがえする	to change money
		… ◇ …	
	着替える	きがえる	to change clothes

30 続 — continue
つづ・く、ゾク

Stroke order: く 乡 幺 糸 糸 糸 糸 糸 糸 紀 紀 続 続 続

Thread 糸 and sell 売 combined, 続 means to continue.

続く	つづく	to continue
手続き	てつづき	procedures
… ◇ …		
続出する	ぞくしゅつする	to appear one after another

31 待 — wait
ま・つ、タイ

Stroke order: ノ ク 彳 彳 彳 彳 待 待 待

The temple was the community center in ancient China, so go 彳 and temple 寺 combined, 待 came to mean to wait for someone at the temple; thus simply to wait.

待つ	まつ	to wait
… ◇ …		
期待する	きたいする	to expect

32 合 — fit; put together
あ・う、ゴウ

Stroke order: ノ 入 合 合 合 合

合 is a pictograph of a lid, and 口 is a hole. Thus 合 means to put together or fit.

待合室	まちあいしつ	waiting room
合う	あう	to fit
話し合う	はなしあう	to discuss
… ◇ …		
組合	くみあい	union
会合	かいごう	meeting
合計	ごうけい	total

| 33 荷 | load; luggage, cargo | 一 | 十 | ヰ | 艹 | 芢 | 芢 | 荷 | 荷 |
| | に | 荷 | 荷 | | | | | | |

A man イ carrying a balance 可 and 艹 plant, 荷 means a load or luggage.

荷物	にもつ	luggage
手荷物	てにもつ	baggage
	… ◇ …	
重荷	おもに	load

| 34 関 | barrier | 丨 | 冂 | 冂 | 冃 | 冃 | 門 | 門 | 門 |
| | カン | 門 | 門 | 閂 | 閈 | 関 | 関 | | |

Gate 門 and barricade 关 combined, 関 means a barrier or barrier station.

税関	ぜいかん	toll
関東	かんとう	Kanto (region)
関西	かんさい	Kansai (region)
	… ◇ …	
関心	かんしん	interest
関税	かんぜい	customs duty

| 35 到 | arrive, reach | 一 | 五 | 云 | 云 | 至 | 至 | 到 | 到 |
| | トウ | | | | | | | | |

到 combines sword リ and reach 至.

| 到着ロビー | とうちゃくロビー | arrival lobby |
| | … ◇ … | |

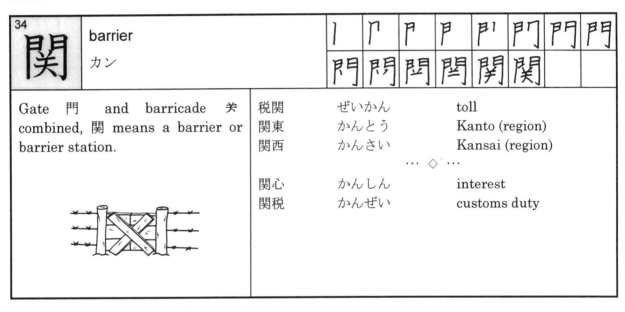

4 PRACTICE

Ⅰ. Write the readings of the following kanji in hiragana.

1. 空 港　　　　　　　2. 旅 客　　　　　　　3. 両 替

4. 免 税　　　　　　　5. 手 荷 物

6. 税関で、手続きをします。

7. 銀行で、円をドルに替えます。

8. 待合室で、すこし休みます。

9. 到着ロビーで、待っています。

10. 旅を続けます。

11. 税金をはらいます。

Ⅱ. Fill in the blanks with appropriate kanji.

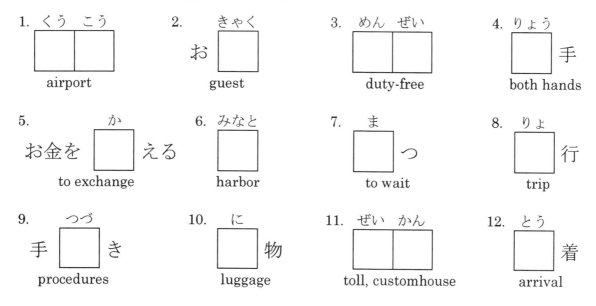

1. くう こう
airport

2. きゃく
お ☐
guest

3. めん ぜい
duty-free

4. りょう
☐ 手
both hands

5. か
お金を ☐ える
to exchange

6. みなと
harbor

7. ま
☐ つ
to wait

8. りょ
☐ 行
trip

9. つづ
手 ☐ き
procedures

10. に
☐ 物
luggage

11. ぜい かん
toll, customhouse

12. とう
☐ 着
arrival

47

Sukiyaki Donburi　すき焼き丼

Directions

＜Warming in boiling water＞

① Put the packet into boiling water and leave it for 5–7 minutes.

② Open the packet and pour it over hot cooked rice in a bowl (about 250g per serving).
A delicious Kobe *sukiyaki donburi* is ready.

▼Caution:　Open the packet carefully.　It is very hot after being boiled.

＜Warming in a microwave oven＞

Empty the contents of the packet into a bowl and heat it covered with plastic wrap.　Refer to the manual for heating time.

(approximate heating time:　2 minutes　500w)

▼Caution:　Do not heat the packet.　It could ignite or explode.

Remove the wrap carefully.

Be careful, the heated soup and ingredients may splash.

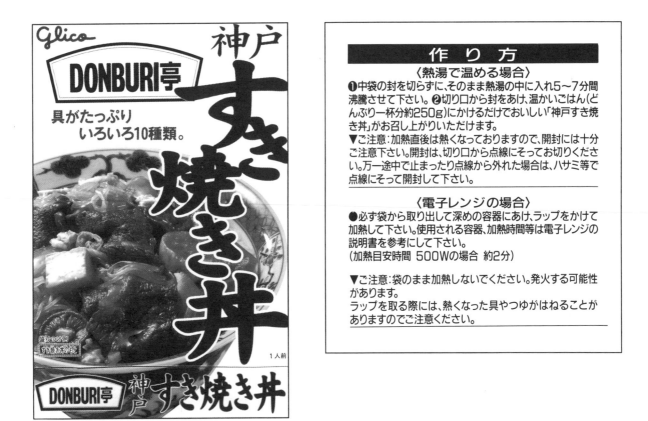

作 り 方

〈熱湯で温める場合〉
❶中袋の封を切らずに、そのまま熱湯の中に入れ5〜7分間沸騰させて下さい。❷切り口から封をあけ、温かいごはん(どんぶり一杯分約250g)にかけるだけでおいしい「神戸すき焼き丼」がお召し上がりいただけます。
▼ご注意:加熱直後は熱くなっておりますので、開封には十分ご注意下さい。開封は、切り口から点線にそってお切りください。万一途中で止まったり点線から外れた場合は、ハサミ等で点線にそって開封して下さい。

〈電子レンジの場合〉
●必ず袋から取り出して深めの容器にあけ、ラップをかけて加熱して下さい。使用される容器、加熱時間等は電子レンジの説明書を参考にして下さい。
(加熱目安時間　500Wの場合　約2分)

▼ご注意:袋のまま加熱しないでください。発火する可能性があります。
ラップを取る際には、熱くなった具やつゆがはねることがありますのでご注意ください。

外国人登録を変更します

Application for a Change of Alien Registration

WHEN THERE are changes in your residence status, such as your place of residence or your employer, or when you extend your period of stay, you must contact the local ward or city office. Changes in status and extensions of stay must be recorded in the Certificate of Alien Registration by using the Application for Registration of Alteration of Registered Items. In this lesson, you will learn how to complete this form.

1 INTRODUCTORY QUIZ

Look at the illustration below and refer to the words in VOCABULARY. Then try the following quiz.

When Mike and Mary moved to a new apartment, they had to inform the local ward office （区役所） of their new address. Mike filled in an APPLICATION FOR REGISTRATION OF ALTERATION OF REGISTERED ITEMS at his ward office.   Fill in the form as Mike did.

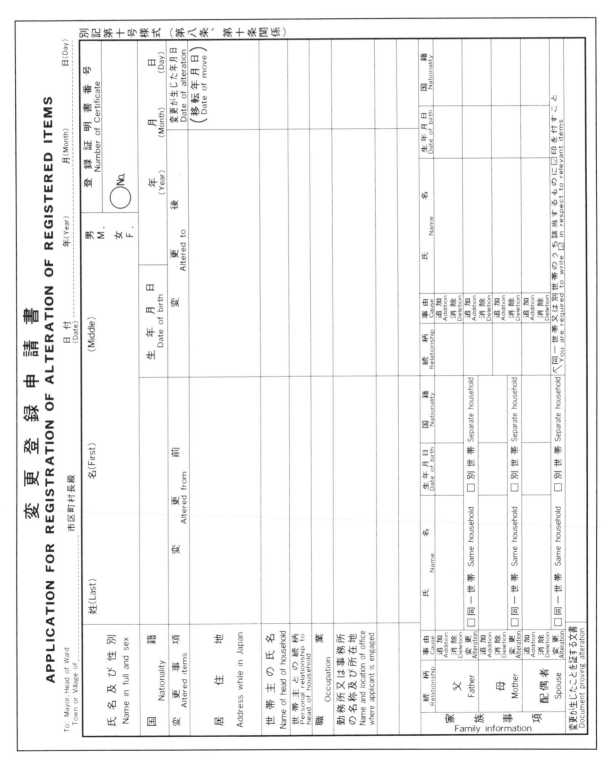

2 VOCABULARY

Study the readings and meanings of these words to help you understand the INTRODUCTORY QUIZ.

1.	変更	へん こう	alteration
2.	登録	とう ろく	registration
3.	申請書	しん せい しょ	application
4.	姓	せい	last name
5.	登録証明書番号	とう ろく しょう めい しょ ばん ごう	certificate number
6.	変更事項	へん こう じ こう	altered items
7.	居住地	きょ じゅう ち	place of residence; address while in Japan
8.	職業	しょく ぎょう	occupation
9.	配偶者	はい ぐう しゃ	spouse
10.	父	ちち	father
11.	母	はは	mother
12.	同一世帯	どう いつ せ たい	same household
13.	別世帯	べつ せ たい	separate household
14.	市役所	し やく しょ	city office

3 NEW CHARACTERS

Ten characters are introduced in this lesson.   Use the explanations to help you understand and remember the characters.   Study the compound words to increase your vocabulary.

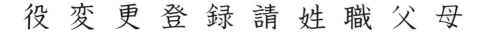

役 変 更 登 録 請 姓 職 父 母

36 役 — service; role
ヤク

ノ ク 彳 彳 役 役 役

役 combines go 彳 and the figure of a weapon 殳, and originally meant to go someplace and fight. 役 then evolved to mean to work, because fighting was the most important kind of work in ancient times. It is used for work, war, and role.

市役所	しやくしょ	city office
区役所	くやくしょ	ward office
役に立つ	やくにたつ	to be useful
… ◇ …		
役目	やくめ	role
役人	やくにん	public officer
主役	しゅやく	principal role

37 変 — change
か・わる、か・える、ヘン

丶 一 ナ ナ 亦 亦 変
変

The upper part 亦 shows tangled thread, compared to the straight warp of a loom, suggesting an unusual situation. 夂 is a trailing leg. If the legs get tangled when walking, it is not an ordinary condition. Thus 変 means change or strange.

変わる	かわる	to change
変える	かえる	to change
大変な	たいへんな	terrible
… ◇ …		
変な人	へんなひと	peculiar person
不変の	ふへんの	unchangeable

38 更 — anew, again
コウ

一 𠀋 𠂤 𠀋 百 更 更

The sun 日 and people 人 begin anew each 一 day. Thus 更 means to renew.

変更する	へんこうする	to change
更新する	こうしんする	to renew, to update
… ◇ …		
更衣室	こういしつ	changing (dressing) room

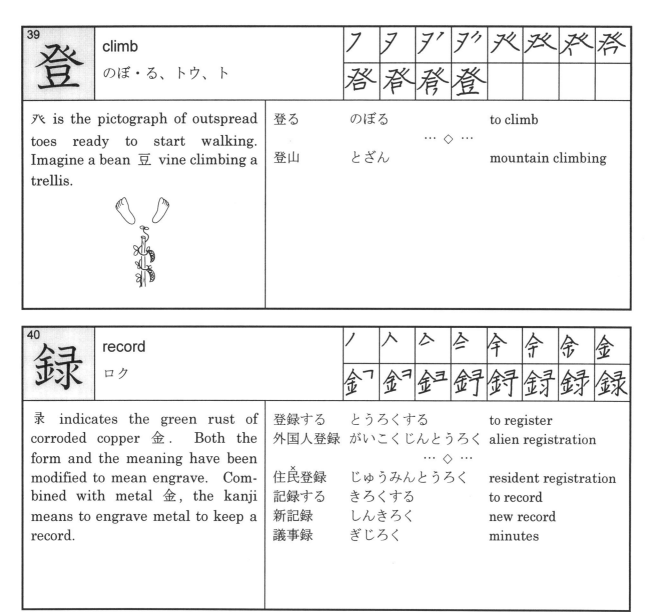

39 登 climb
のぼ・る、トウ、ト

ア ヲ ヺ ヺ 癶 癶 癶 癶
癶 癶 癶 登

癶 is the pictograph of outspread toes ready to start walking. Imagine a bean 豆 vine climbing a trellis.

登る	のぼる	to climb
	… ◇ …	
登山	とざん	mountain climbing

40 録 record
ロク

ノ 入 ㅅ 合 今 令 金 金
金ㄱ 金ㅋ 金ㅋ 釒 釒 釒 録 録

录 indicates the green rust of corroded copper 金. Both the form and the meaning have been modified to mean engrave. Combined with metal 金, the kanji means to engrave metal to keep a record.

登録する	とうろくする	to register
外国人登録	がいこくじんとうろく	alien registration
	… ◇ …	
住民登録	じゅうみんとうろく	resident registration
記録する	きろくする	to record
新記録	しんきろく	new record
議事録	ぎじろく	minutes

41 請 ask for; receive
セイ

丶 亠 ゠ 言 言 言 言 言
訁 訁 訐 請 請 請 請

Transparent 青 and say 言 together mean to say things frankly or to plead earnestly.

申請書	しんせいしょ	application form
申請する	しんせいする	to apply
	… ◇ …	
請求書	せいきゅうしょ	bill
請求する	せいきゅうする	to demand

42 姓 — family name / セイ

く	タ	女	女'	女⺊	女⺮	女⺀	姓

In ancient China, women 女 carried down the family names from generation 生 to generation. Thus 姓 means family name.

姓	せい	family name
姓名	せいめい	full name

… ◇ …

43 職 — occupation / ショク

一	丁	F	F	巨	耳	耳'	耳⺀
耴	耵	耶	聕	職	職	職	

In ancient China, professional soldiers used daggers 戈 and they listened 耳 attentively to the sounds 音 around them when fighting. As this activity represented their employment, 職 came to mean occupation.

職	しょく	job
職業	しょくぎょう	occupation

… ◇ …

職員	しょくいん	staff (member)
無職	むしょく	no occupation
休職	きゅうしょく	on leave
内職	ないしょく	job on the side

44 父 — father / ちち、フ

ノ	ハ	父	父				

As mature men in the family were traditionally responsible for wood cutting, a hand 乂 with an ax signifies father.

父	ちち	father

… ◇ …

義父	ぎふ	father-in-law

45 母	mother はは、ボ	人	勹	勾	身	母			

A human figure with pronounced breasts suggests nursing; thus this kanji means mother.

母	はは	mother
父母	ふぼ	father and mother; parents
母の日	ははのひ	Mother's Day
	‥‥ ◇ ‥‥	
生母	せいぼ	one's real mother

4 PRACTICE

Ⅰ. Write the readings of the following kanji in hiragana.

  1. 変　更　　　　　2. 登　録　　　　　3. 申　請　書　　　　　4. 姓　名

  5. 職　業　　　　　6. 父　母

  7. この本は、役に立ちます。

  8. 母は、山に登るのが大変好きです。

  9. オリンピックで、新記録が出ました。

  10. 自宅の住所が、変わりました。

  11. 家のちかくに、市役所も区役所もあります。

Ⅱ. Fill in the blanks with appropriate kanji.

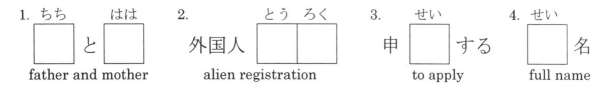

1. ちち　はは
□ と □
father and mother

2. とう　ろく
外国人 □ □
alien registration

3. せい
申 □ する
to apply

4. せい
□ 名
full name

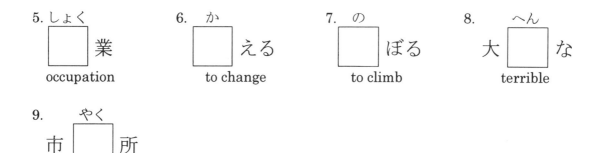

5. しょく
☐業
occupation

6. か
☐える
to change

7. の
☐ぼる
to climb

8. へん
大☐な
terrible

9. やく
市☐所
city office

5 SUPPLEMENT

Signs at the Ward Office

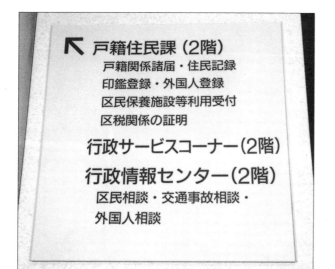

Family Registration (2F)
  Seal Registration
  Alien Registration

Administration Service Corner (2F)
Administration Information Center (2F)
  Japanese and Foreign Residents
  Traffic Accidents

Alien Registration

きょうはなにが安いですか

Shopping at a Supermarket

IN JAPAN, supermarkets are proliferating in the suburbs and near large public housing projects. Supermarkets are convenient for the many services they offer. In addition to shopping, one can stop for a light meal, have photographs developed, take advantage of home delivery services, have gifts wrapped, access copying machines, and more. For this reason, supermarkets are an important part of daily life. *Konbini,* or convenience stores, on the other hand, are a "must" for those who keep late hours. In addition to the regular services of a supermarket, convenience stores offer 24-hour bill payment or movie-ticket purchases, all long after regular office hours.

1 INTRODUCTORY QUIZ

Look at the illustrations below and refer to the words in VOCABULARY. Then try the following quiz.

Below are excerpts from Japanese supermarket flyers. Which items are a good bargain? Can you find the following kanji words?

1. 半 額   2. 特 価   3. 牛 乳   4. 冷 凍 食 品
5. 塩   6. 直 送   7. ２ 枚 組   8. お 買 得

2 VOCABULARY

Study the readings and meanings of these words to help you understand the INTRODUC-TORY QUIZ.

1.	半額	はん がく	half price
2.	特価	とっ か	special price, bargain price
3.	牛乳	ぎゅう にゅう	milk
4.	冷凍食品	れい とう しょく ひん	frozen food
5.	うす塩	うす じお	lightly salted
6.	直送	ちょく そう	direct delivery
7.	３枚組	さん まい ぐみ	three-in-a-set, triple pack
8.	お買い得	お か い どく	bargain

3 NEW CHARACTERS

Eleven characters are introduced in this lesson. Use the explanations to help you understand and remember the characters. Study the compound words to increase your vocabulary.

額 価 得 乳 冷 凍 塩 直 送 枚 組

46 額	amount ガク	¹ ｜ 宀 宀 宀 宽 客 客 客 客 客 額 額 額

The number or head count 頁 of guests 客 suggests the amount of money needed to entertain them.	半額	はんがく	half price
	金額	きんがく	sum of money
	全額	ぜんがく	full price
	… ◇ …		
	小額	しょうがく	small sum of money

47 価

price; value

カ

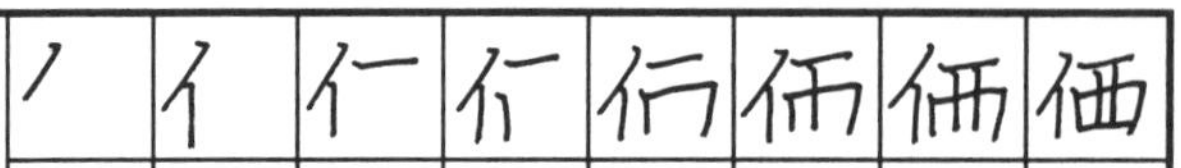

価 is the selling price of the goods that a merchant or person イ stored in a warehouse.

特価	とっか	bargain
定価	ていか	retail price
物価	ぶっか	commodity price

… ◇ …

価格	かかく	price
原価	げんか	cost price

48 得

gain

トク、（ドク）

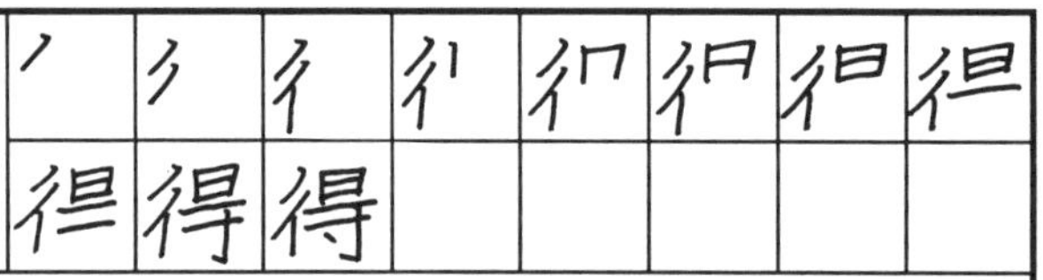

Go 彳 to catch shellfish 旦 by hand 寸 means to catch something valuable, or to gain something.

買(い)得	かいどく	bargain

… ◇ …

得意な	とくいな	be good at
お得意さま	おとくいさま	customer
所得	しょとく	income

49 乳

milk

ニュウ

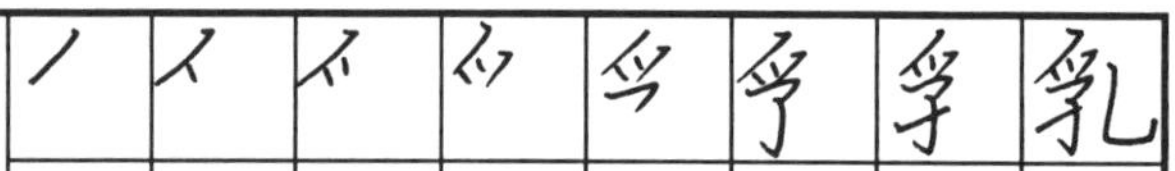

A mother's hand ⺥ holding her child 子 against her breast L forms the kanji for milk.

牛乳	ぎゅうにゅう	milk
母乳	ぼにゅう	mother's milk

… ◇ …

50 冷

cold, chill

つめ・たい、レイ

丶	ン	ソ	ソ	冫	冷	冷

冫 means ice. 令 is added for pronunciation. Thus 冷 means icy cold, or chilly.

冷たい	つめたい	cold
	… ◇ …	
冷房	れいぼう	air conditioning
冷水	れいすい	cold water
冷蔵する	れいぞうする	to keep (food) cool

51 凍

frozen

トウ

丶	ン	冫	汀	沪	洰	洰	凍
凍	凍						

冫 means ice. So together with 東, meaning east, from which the cold winds blow, the kanji means frozen.

冷凍食品	れいとうしょくひん	frozen food
	… ◇ …	
不凍港	ふとうこう	ice-free port
凍結する	とうけつする	to freeze

52 塩

salt

しお、エン

一	十	土	圡	圹	圬	坧	垍
垍	塩	塩	塩	塩			

A man eats salt from the ground 土 with his mouth 口 using a plate 皿.

塩	しお	salt
塩水	しおみず	salty water
	… ◇ …	
塩分	えんぶん	salinity

53 直 direct; honest, frank
チョク、（チョッ）

一 ナ ナ 方 方 直 直 直

Many 十 eyes 目 in a corner ∟ mean to be straight, direct, or to repair and correct, because when a family has a problem, family members get together to solve it.

直通電話	ちょくつうでんわ	direct line
直行便	ちょっこうびん	direct flight
	… ◇ …	
直線	ちょくせん	straight line
直前	ちょくぜん	just before
直後	ちょくご	just after

54 送 send
おく・る、ソウ

丶 ゛ ′ ′ ′ 关 关 送

送

关 is the pictograph of holding things with both hands. With to move onward 辶, 送 means to send.

送る	おくる	to send
見送る	みおくる	to see off
産地直送	さんちちょくそう	sent directly from the producer
送料	そうりょう	delivery charge
	… ◇ …	
送別会	そうべつかい	farewell party
運送会社	うんそうがいしゃ	shipping agency

55 枚 counter for a thin flat object
マイ

一 十 オ 木 木 枚 枚 枚

枚 combines tree 木 and a hand holding a plank 攵. 枚 is used to count any kind of flat object.

一枚	いちまい	one sheet
	… ◇ …	
枚数	まいすう	number of sheets
大枚	たいまい	large sum of money

56 組	group; put together	く	幺	幺	糸	弁	糸	糹	糸
	くみ、（ぐみ）	糸	絔	組					

By combining thread 糸 and to pile up 且, 組 means to form something larger by making a cord out of many threads.	二枚組	にまいぐみ	set of two
	大木組	おおきぐみ	Oki Corporation
		… ◇ …	
	番組	ばんぐみ	(TV) program
	組み立てる	くみたてる	to assemble
	組み合わせる	くみあわせる	to combine

4　PRACTICE

Ⅰ. Write the readings of the following kanji in hiragana.

1. 半　額　　　2. 特　価　　3. 送　料　　4. 塩　分　　5. 冷　凍

6. 塩　　　　　7. 直　送　　8. 二　枚　組

9. 冷たい牛乳が、飲みたいです。

10. 日本は、物価が高いです。

11. シャツを三枚、おくります。

12. 定価の３割引ですから、お買い得です。

Ⅱ. Fill in the blanks with appropriate kanji.

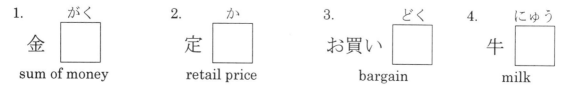

1. がく 金 ☐ sum of money	2. か 定 ☐ retail price	3. どく お買い ☐ bargain	4. にゅう 牛 ☐ milk

5. れい とう

□□ 食品

frozen food

6. ちょく そう

産地 □□

sent directly from the producer

7. まい ぐみ

二 □□

set of two

8. ちょく

□ 行便

direct flight

9. しお

□

salt

10. おく

□ る

to send

11. つめ

□ たい

cold

5 | SUPPLEMENT

Signs at the Convenience Store

NHK_{じゅしんりょうまどぐち}受信料窓口   NHK fee payment

<ruby>電話料金窓口<rt>でんわりょうきんまどぐち</rt></ruby>   telephone bill payment

<ruby>国際電話料金窓口<rt>こくさいでんわりょうきんまどぐち</rt></ruby>   international telephone bill payment

<ruby>電気料金窓口<rt>でんきりょうきんまどぐち</rt></ruby>   electricity bill payment

<ruby>ガス料金窓口<rt>りょうきんまどぐち</rt></ruby>   gas bill payment

<ruby>保険料窓口<rt>ほけんりょうまどぐち</rt></ruby>   insurance premium payment

<ruby>宅急便<rt>たっきゅうびん</rt></ruby>   home delivery

<ruby>酒類<rt>さけるい</rt></ruby>   liquor

ちかくの店で買います

Strolling Along a Shopping Street

SHOPPING STREETS surround most neighborhoods and supplement the goods offered by supermarkets. In the small stores that line the shopping streets, shop owners are happy to talk with you and answer questions about their goods as well as about activities in the area in general. Shopkeepers usually belong to a community organization called the *shotengai* or *shotenkai,* which promotes their business. Special sale events are often held on shopping streets, especially during the summer and at the end of the year. Shopkeepers are likely to offer frequent-shopper coupons or discounts to encourage residents to shop in the neighborhood regularly. In this lesson, you will learn the names of many specialty shops likely to be found on a shopping street.

1 INTRODUCTORY QUIZ

Look at the illustrations below and refer to the words in VOCABULARY. Then try the following quiz.

Mary's Japanese neighbor took her around a shopping street and showed her the services available from a wide range of specialty stores.

Where should she or her family go for the following services? Fill in the spaces with the correct letters (a～k) of shops.

1. しゃしんを取る　　　　　　　　　　　　　　　　（　　　）
2. ノートや、えんぴつや、ふうとうを買う　　　　　（　　　）
3. かるい食事をして、コーヒーを飲む　　　　　　　（　　　）
4. おこめを買う　　　　　　　　　　　　　　　　　（　　　）
5. いろいろなおさけを買う　　　　　　　　　　　　（　　　）
6. ふるい本を買う　　　　　　　　　　　　　　　　（　　　）
7. メアリーさんが、かみ*をセットする　　（*hair）　（　　　）
8. トムさんが、ともだちとおさけを飲みに行く　　　（　　　）
9. はなを買う　　　　　　　　　　　　　　　　　　（　　　）
10. トムさんが、かみをみじかくする　　　　　　　　（　　　）
11. やきにくを食べる　　　　　　　　　　　　　　　（　　　）

2 VOCABULARY

Study the readings and meanings of these words to help you understand the INTRODUC-TORY QUIZ.

1.	商店街	しょう てん がい	shopping street
2.	写真	しゃ しん	photograph
3.	証明写真	しょう めい しゃ しん	instant photo machine
4.	文具（店）	ぶん ぐ（てん）	stationery; a stationery store
5.	花店	はな てん	flower shop
6.	米（屋）	こめ（や）	rice shop, rice store
7.	酒（屋）	さか（や）	liquor store
8.	居酒屋	い ざか や	bar, pub
9.	古本（屋）	ふる ほん（や）	secondhand bookstore/bookseller
10.	美容室	び よう しつ	beauty salon/parlor
11.	年中無休	ねん じゅう む きゅう	open year-round
12.	営業時間	えい ぎょう じ かん	business hours
13.	理容（店）	り よう（てん）	barbershop; barber
14.	焼肉レストラン	やき にく レストラン	*yakiniku* restaurant
15.	軽食	けい しょく	snack, light meal
16.	喫茶	きっ さ	coffee shop

3 NEW CHARACTERS

Eleven characters are introduced in this lesson. Use the explanations to help you understand and remember the characters. Study the compound words to increase your vocabulary.

写 真 具 花 米 酒 古 美 容 焼 軽

57 写 copy, duplicate うつ・す、シャ	ノ 冖 宀 写 写				

Cover 冖 joined with give 与 leads to the kanji for copy 写, as in "I will give you copies of the pictures I took."	写す うつす to copy, to photograph
	··· ◇ ···
	写生する しゃせいする to sketch

58 真 truth, reality; exactly ま、シン	一 ナ 十 方 方 有 直 直 真 真							

Antenna 十, eyes 目, and table 八 combined resemble a TV set, which shows real pictures or images.	真上 まうえ right above
	写真 しゃしん photograph
	··· ◇ ···
	真理 しんり truth
	真空 しんくう vacuum

59 具 — tool — グ

丨	冂	冃	月	目	目	具	具	

A container 目 held with both hands 廾 represents a useful, even vital utensil.

文具	ぶんぐ	stationery
家具	かぐ	furniture

··· ◇ ···

道具	どうぐ	tool
実験器具	じっけんきぐ	equipment for laboratory use

60 花 — flower — はな

一	十	艹	艻	芢	花	花	

化 means change and plant 艹 is added to get 花, which means a flower that will eventually change into seed.

花	はな	flower
花屋	はなや	florist

··· ◇ ···

61 米 — rice; America — こめ、ベイ

丶	丷	丷	半	米	米	

It takes eighty-eight 八十八 processes before we can eat rice. Another explanation says that 米 is the pictograph of a grain.

米屋	こめや	rice store
米国	べいこく	United States of America
中南米	ちゅうなんべい	South and Central America

··· ◇ ···

62 酒	wine, rice wine *(sake)*, liquor さけ、（さか）、（ざか）、シュ	丶	亅	氵	汀	汀	沔	沔	酒
		酒	酒						

酉 is the pictograph of a wine jar with water 氵 added for emphasis.

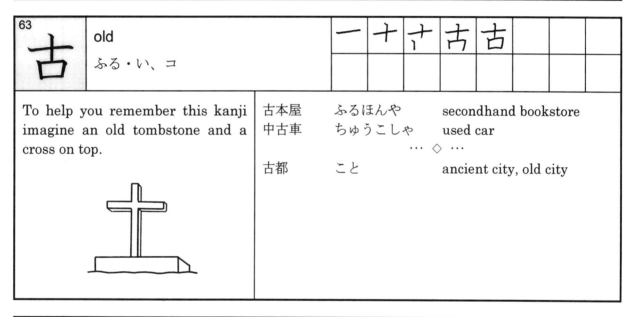

酒	さけ	liquor
酒屋	さかや	liquor store
日本酒	にほんしゅ	Japanese rice wine *(sake)*
	… ◇ …	
居酒屋	いざかや	bar, pub
禁酒	きんしゅ	abstinence from alcohol
酒場	さかば	bar

63 古	old ふる・い、コ	一	十	十	古	古			

To help you remember this kanji imagine an old tombstone and a cross on top.

古本屋	ふるほんや	secondhand bookstore
中古車	ちゅうこしゃ	used car
	… ◇ …	
古都	こと	ancient city, old city

64 美	beautiful うつく・しい、ビ	丶	丷	艹	兰	兰	羊	羊	羊
		美							

Sheep 羊 and big 大 together means beautiful, because sheep were very important for the ancient Chinese. Big sheep are thought to be very beautiful.

美しい	うつくしい	beautiful
美人	びじん	beautiful woman
	… ◇ …	
人工美	じんこうび	manmade beauty

65 容 contain; form, appearance
ヨウ

ﾉ　ｿ　宀　宀　宍　夵　夵　宨
容　容

House 宀 and valley 谷 together 容 means to put something in place.

美容室	びようしつ	beauty parlor
美容院	びよういん	beauty shop
内容	ないよう	content
… ◇ …		
容量	ようりょう	capacity
容積	ようせき	bulk

---

66 焼 burn; roast, bake
や・く、や・ける

ﾉ　ｿ　ｿ　火　灼　灯　灶　焒
焒　焼　焼　焼

尭 looks like piled-up timbers on a stand. 火 is added to signify a flame burning intensely.

焼く	やく	to burn, roast, bake, grill
焼き肉	やきにく	grilled meat
すき焼き	すきやき	*sukiyaki*
焼き鳥	やきとり	grilled chicken on skewers
… ◇ …		
焼ける	やける	to be burned, to be roasted, to be grilled
夕焼け	ゆうやけ	colors of the sunset

---

67 軽 light; easy
かる・い、ケイ

一　厂　斤　斤　百　車　車　軒
軒　軽　軽　軽

圣 is the pictograph of a loom with a straight warp, and when it is combined with vehicle 車, it implies something which moves straight and easily, much as a loom with a straight warp moves easily.

軽い	かるい	light
軽食	けいしょく	light meal
… ◇ …		
軽工業	けいこうぎょう	light industry
軽音楽	けいおんがく	light music

4 PRACTICE

Ⅰ. Write the readings of the following kanji in hiragana.

1. 文具　　　2. 酒　　　3. 軽食　　　4. 古本屋

5. 内容　　　6. 古い　　　7. 美しい

8. 写真を三枚、写しました。

9. 日本酒は、米からつくられます。

10. 毎月、美容院へ行きます。

11. 焼肉も焼き鳥も、おいしいです。

12. 中古車は、新車より安いです。

13. この家具は、軽くて、じょうぶです。

14. 花屋さんで、バラを十本買いました。

Ⅱ. Fill in the blanks with appropriate kanji.

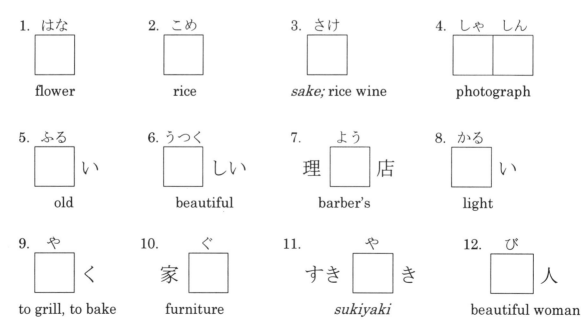

1. はな
flower

2. こめ
rice

3. さけ
sake; rice wine

4. しゃ しん
photograph

5. ふる　い
old

6. うつく　しい
beautiful

7. 理 よう 店
barber's

8. かる　い
light

9. や　く
to grill, to bake

10. 家 ぐ
furniture

11. すき や き
sukiyaki

12. び 人
beautiful woman

ゴミの出し方

Putting Out the Garbage

GARBAGE COLLECTION is regulated by the local governmental garbage collection department, *Seisojimusho*. This means that the rules differ from prefecture to prefecture. In Tokyo, combustible garbage is collected three days a week and noncombustible garbage is collected once a week. Collection days are decided by a local office and differ by area. Large items like furniture are collected twice a month by appointment with the office in your area. Nowadays, recycling is encouraged. Cans and bottles are collected on a certain day of the week, while paper and clothing are collected once a month. Big supermarkets or local city offices often provide recycling bins near the front entrance for the disposal of plastic wrappings and milk cartons. These recycling programs are sponsored by the local governmental office or are on a voluntary basis. In this lesson, you will learn the kanji associated with garbage disposal.

1 INTRODUCTORY QUIZ

Look at the illustration below and refer to the words in VOCABULARY. Then try the following quiz.

The Japanese woman who lives next door to Mary showed her when to throw away garbage and those things she does not need anymore.

ゴミの正しい分け方・出し方			
区　分	可 燃 ゴ ミ	不燃（分別）ゴミ	粗 大 ゴ ミ
	週3回　月・水・金	週1回　土曜日	申し込み制（電話をかけて下さい）
分け方	生 ゴ ミ 紙　類 衣　類	び　ん プラスチック類 缶 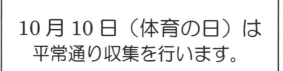	い　す テーブル テ レ ビ

When is the next collection day? When is the appropriate day of the week to dispose of an item, or for what do you have to make an appointment ahead of time by phone? Fill in the spaces with the correct letters (a〜c).

1. プラスチックのびん　　　　　（　　　）
2. 古くなったテレビ　　　　　　（　　　）
3. やさい　　　　　　　　　　　（　　　）
4. ジュースの空き缶　　　　　　（　　　）
5. てがみ　　　　　　　　　　　（　　　）
6. カップラーメンの入れ物　　　（　　　）

a	月・水・金曜日
b	土曜日
c	電話で申し込みます

Note: Sometimes you will see a notice at the garbage collection point.

お願い ゴミは指定日以外に 出さないで下さい。	10月10日（体育の日）は 平常通り収集を行います。
指定日以外の日には出さないでください。	平常通り収集を行います。
Please do not throw out garbage on the wrong day.	Garbage collection will continue as usual on October 10, a national holiday.

2 VOCABULARY

Study the readings and meanings of these words to help you understand the INTRODUC-
TORY QUIZ.

1.	ゴミ容器	ゴミ ようき	garbage container
2.	集積所	しゅう せき しょ	collection point
3.	収集日	しゅう しゅう び	collection days
4.	区分	く ぶん	sorting, classification
5.	可燃ゴミ（普通ゴミ）	か ねん ゴミ （ふ つう ゴミ）	combustible garbage
6.	不燃ゴミ（分別ゴミ）	ふ ねん ゴミ （ぶん べつ ゴミ）	noncombustible garbage
7.	粗大ゴミ	そ だい ゴミ	outsized trash
8.	申込み制	もうし こ み せい	contact the garbage collection office
9.	生ゴミ	なま ゴミ	food scraps
10.	紙類	かみ るい	paper
11.	衣類	い るい	clothing
12.	びん		bottles
13.	缶	かん	cans
14.	お願い	お ねが い	request
15.	指定日以外	し てい び い がい	noncollection days
16.	平常通り	へい じょう どお り	as usual
17.	行う	おこな う	to do

3 NEW CHARACTERS

Twelve characters are introduced in this lesson. Use the explanations to help you
understand and remember the characters. Study the compound words to increase your
vocabulary.

器 積 収 可 燃 粗 制 類 願 指 以 缶

68 器	container; apparatus	キ	⼁	⼌	口	叩	叩	叩	哭	哭
			哭	哭	器	器	器	器	器	

The old kanji 器 was a combination of four mouths 口 and a dog 犬, meaning a plate with dog's meat eaten by four mouths. Now 器 means a simple machine or a container.

容器	ようき	container
食器	しょっき	tableware
	… ◇ …	
消火器	しょうかき	fire extinguisher
楽器	がっき	musical instrument
受話器	じゅわき	telephone receiver
器用な	きような	skillful

69 積	heap up, load, accumulate	セキ	ノ	⼆	千	千	禾	禾	禾	禾
			秸	秸	積	積	積	積	積	積

This kanji means to accumulate, which you can remember by imagining a pile of grain 禾 you accumulate when neighbors come to repay their debts 貝 to you.

ゴミ集積所	ゴミしゅうせきじょ	garbage collection place
	… ◇ …	
面積	めんせき	space
体積	たいせき	volume

70 収	obtain, collect	シュウ	⼁	4	収	収				

Two strings 丩 and a hand 又 create the image of a hand gathering separate things into one. Thus 収 means to gather or collect.

収集日	しゅうしゅうび	collection day
収入	しゅうにゅう	income
月収	げっしゅう	monthly income
	… ◇ …	
収容人数	しゅうようにんずう	number of persons to be accommodated
ゴミの回収	ゴミのかいしゅう	garbage collection

71 可	good; possible; can; approval カ	一	丁	〒	可	可			

可 is the pictograph of a crooked throat and a mouth, suggesting that the sound meaning "can" comes from a tensed, constricted throat. Thus 可 means can or approve.

可と不可	かとふか	pass and fail
	… ◇ …	
可決	かけつ	approval (of a proposed law)

72 燃	burn も・える、ネン	、	丷	少	火	火	灼	炒	烂
		炒一	炒ｸ	火炒	炒犬	燃犬	燃	燃	燃

Meat 月 and dog 犬 combine with fire 火 and flame 灬, the nature of fire, to burn.

燃えるゴミ	もえるゴミ	combustible garbage
可燃ゴミ	かねんゴミ	combustible garbage
不燃ゴミ	ふねんゴミ	noncombustible garbage
燃料	ねんりょう	fuel
	… ◇ …	

73 粗	coarse, rough ソ	、	丷	丷	半	半	米	籵	籵
		粗	粗	粗					

Coarse 且 and rice 米 combine so that 粗 means coarse rice. Today, 粗 has evolved to mean coarse or rough.

粗大ゴミ	そだいゴミ	outsized trash
	… ◇ …	
粗食	そしょく	plain diet
粗野な	そやな	vulgar, rustic

74

制

regulate; system

セイ

𠂒 is a pictograph of a tree being cut in the middle to make lumber, and when sword 刂 is added, they combine to mean to regulate or a system.

申込み制	もうしこみせい	upon application
	… ◇ …	
制度	せいど	system
税制	ぜいせい	taxation system
強制	きょうせい	compulsion

75

類

rice

ルイ

Rice 米 is categorized according to the size (大 or 小) of the grain head 頁.

人類	じんるい	mankind
書類	しょるい	papers, documents
	… ◇ …	
衣類	いるい	clothing
紙類	かみるい	paper
分類する	ぶんるいする	to categorize
類語	るいご	synonym

76

願

wish

ねが・う、ガン

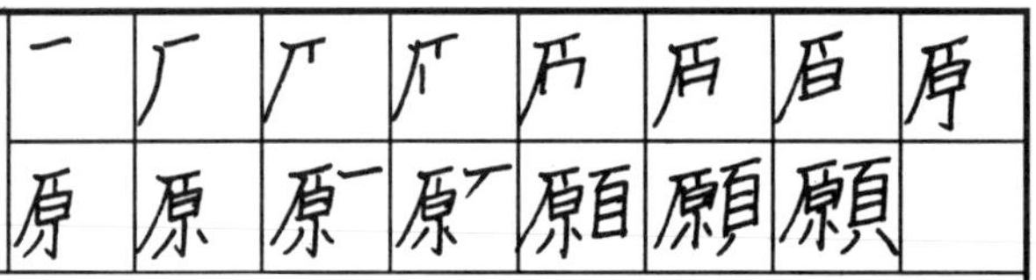

原 is the figure of white 白 clear spring water 小＝水, running at the foot of a cliff 厂. 原 means original, because a spring is the origin of water. Head 頁 is added to mean wish, because the original 原 function of the head 頁 is to ask god for something.

お願い	おねがい	request
願書	がんしょ	application for admission
	… ◇ …	

77 指 — finger; point to
ゆび、シ

一 丁 才 才 扩 扩 指 指
指

日 is a simplified form of sweet 甘 and ヒ is a ladle. Thus 旨 means tasty. By extension, 旨 means good or important. The most important 旨 parts of a hand are fingers.

指	ゆび	finger
指定日	していび	appointed day
… ◇ …		
指定席	していせき	reserved seat
小指	こゆび	little finger
指名する	しめいする	to nominate

78 以 — ~ than (prefix); by means of
イ

丨 丿 㠯 以 以

Two people 以 can do better than one person.

以外	いがい	other than
二人以上	ふたりいじょう	two or more people
三日以内	みっかいない	within three days
… ◇ …		

79 缶 — metal container
カン

丿 ナ 上 午 缶 缶

缶 is the pictograph of a round earthenware jug. Now 缶 means a metal container.

缶	かん	can
缶切り	かんきり	can opener
空き缶	あきかん	empty can
… ◇ …		

4 PRACTICE

I. Write the readings of the following kanji in hiragana.

1. 容 器　　　　2. 集 積 所　　　　3. 収 集 日　　　　4. 可 燃 ゴ ミ

5. 指 定 日　　　　6. 以 外　　　　7. 人 類　　　　8. 指

9. よろしくお願いします。

10. 粗大ゴミは、申し込み制です。

11. 燃えないゴミは、不燃ゴミといいます。

12. 願書に記入します。

13. 空き缶を集めてください。

II. Fill in the blanks with appropriate kanji.

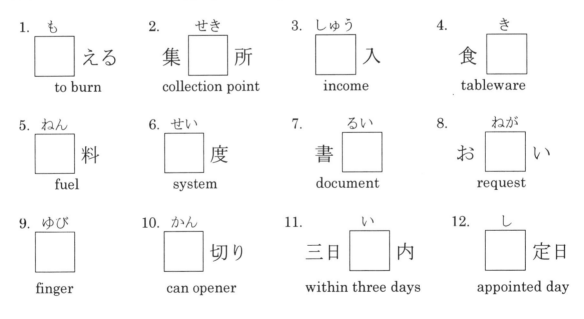

1. も [　] える — to burn

2. せき 集 [　] 所 — collection point

3. しゅう [　] 入 — income

4. き 食 [　] — tableware

5. ねん [　] 料 — fuel

6. せい [　] 度 — system

7. るい 書 [　] — document

8. ねが お [　] い — request

9. ゆび [　] — finger

10. かん [　] 切り — can opener

11. い 三日 [　] 内 — within three days

12. し [　] 定日 — appointed day

ともだちの家へ行きます

Visiting Friends

THERE ARE *jukyo-hyoji-annaizu,* or street maps, posted near stations or street corners in most neighborhoods. The maps are helpful when you want to orient yourself in a new neighborhood, or to find public facilities such as schools, police stations, or post offices. Symbols are used on the maps: 文 means schools, 开 means shrines, 卍 means temples. Evacuation areas (広域避難場所) are also marked. These maps will show you where to assemble in the event of disasters, such as earthquakes or fires. In this lesson you will learn some of the kanji used for the names of the public buildings that are most often featured on such maps.

1 INTRODUCTORY QUIZ

Look at the illustration below and refer to the words in VOCABULARY. Then try the following quiz.

Mr. Kawamura sent Mike and Mary an invitation to his home. They are looking at the *jukyo-hyoji-annaizu* （住居表示案内図） in front of the train station to find Mr. Kawamura's house. Which is his house, a, b, c, or d?

みなさん、お元気ですか。
　来週の土曜日、私の家に来てください。石山町駅から歩いて５〜６分です。
まず、駅前に駐車場と自転車おき場があります。その間を通って、駐車場の
かどを右にまがってください。つぎに、２つ目のかどを左にまがって、もみ
じ川のはしをわたります。そしてすぐに右にまがってください。私の家は、
かどから二つ目です。
　それでは、たのしみにしております。

川村ひろし

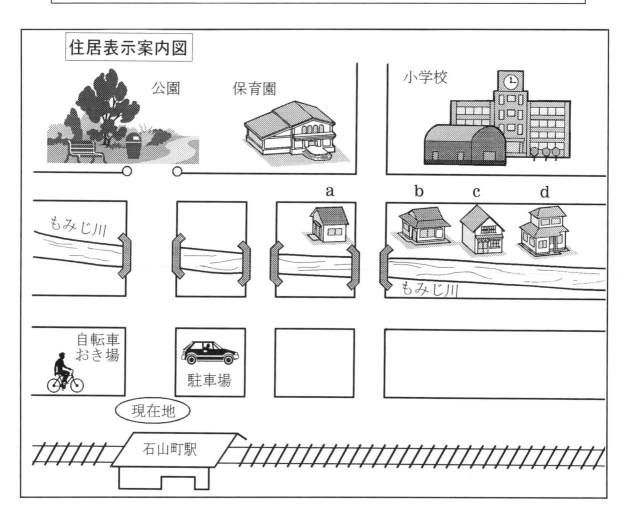

2 VOCABULARY

Study the readings and meanings of these words to help you understand the INTRODUC-TORY QUIZ.

1.	私	わたし	I
2.	石山町	いし やま ちょう	Ishiyama-cho (place name)
3.	駅前	えき まえ	in front of the station
4.	駐車場	ちゅう しゃ じょう	parking lot
5.	もみじ川	もみじ がわ	Momiji River
6.	小学校	しょう がっ こう	elementary school
7.	保育園	ほ いく えん	day nursery
8.	住居表示案内図	じゅう きょ ひょう じ あん ない ず	street map
9.	自転車おき場	じ てん しゃ おき ば	bicycle parking lot
10.	現在地	げん ざい ち	place where one is now

3 NEW CHARACTERS

Twelve characters are introduced in this lesson. Use the explanations to help you understand and remember the characters. Study the compound words to increase your vocabulary.

私 石 町 駐 川 校 育 園 示 村 転 現

80 私	I; private わたくし、（わたし）、シ	ノ 二 千 爿 禾 私 私

禾 is grain. ム is the figure of an arm holding grain. Thus 私 means to take in the grain or whatever belongs to an individual.	私	わたくし	I
	私立	しりつ	private (institution)
	… ◇ …		
	私費で	しひで	at one's own expense
	私用	しよう	private engagement
	私生活	しせいかつ	private life

81 石	stone いし、セキ、（セッ）	一	厂	厂	石	石		

This is the pictograph of a big stone and a cliff combined.	石　　　　いし　　　　　　　stone
	… ◇ …
	石けん　　せっけん　　　　　soap
	石油　　　せきゆ　　　　　　oil
	石庭　　　せきてい　　　　　rock garden

82 町	town; quarter まち、チョウ	1	冂	冂	冊	田	田	町

A rice field 田 and a road 丁 formed a town.	町　　　　　まち　　　　　　　　town, quarter
	大手町　　　おおてまち　　　　　Otemachi (place name)
	有楽町　　　ゆうらくちょう　　　Yurakucho (place name)
	町長　　　　ちょうちょう　　　　mayor of a town
	… ◇ …
	町内会　　　ちょうないかい　　　neighborhood association

83 駐	stop; reside チュウ	一	厂	冂	开	严	馬	馬	馬
		馬	馬	馬`	馬ー	駐	駐	駐	

Horse 馬 and master 主 combined, 駐 refers to a place where ancient Chinese people kept horses. Now 駐 means to park cars or bicycles.	駐車場　　ちゅうしゃじょう　parking lot
	… ◇ …
	駐日大使　ちゅうにちたいし　ambassador to Japan

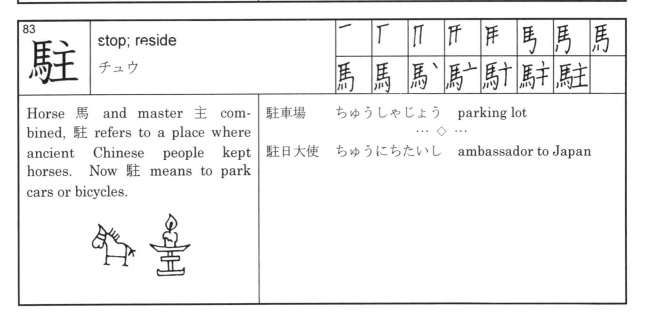

84 川	river かわ、（がわ）	）	）｜	）｜｜				

From an image of a flowing river, the Chinese drew the character for river.	川	かわ	river
	品川	しながわ	Shinagawa (place name)
		… ◇ …	
	川下	かわしも	downstream

85 校	school; (printer's) proof コウ	一	十	才	木	木`	杧	杧	杧
		杈	校						

Schoolhouses built by the ancient Chinese were like log cabins, thus the 木 in 校.	小学校	しょうがっこう	elementary school
	中学校	ちゅうがっこう	junior high school
	高校	こうこう	high school
		… ◇ …	
	母校	ぼこう	alma mater
	校正する	こうせいする	to read proofs
	校長	こうちょう	principal

86 育	to raise; to educate そだ・てる、イク	`	亠	士	云	产	产	育	育

An inverted form of a child 子 suggesting birth, and body 月 meaning an adult, together 育 means to raise children.	育てる	そだてる	to raise
	教育	きょういく	education
		… ◇ …	
	体育	たいいく	physical education
	発育	はついく	growth

87 園	yard その、エン	丨 冂 冃 冃 冃 冃 冃 禸 禸 禸 禸 禸 園

裳 is the pictograph of old-fashioned clothing which is very loose and extends a distance from the body. Combined with 囗, it means a round, enclosed area or a yard.

保育園	ほいくえん	nursery
公園	こうえん	park
動物園	どうぶつえん	zoo
… ◇ …		
植物園	しょくぶつえん	botanical garden
学園	がくえん	educational institution
楽園	らくえん	paradise
園田	そのだ	Sonoda (family name)

88 示	show, indicate しめ・す、ジ	一 二 亍 示 示

This is the pictograph of an altar, representing a shrine. Thus 示 means to reveal or show, because a shrine is the place where god's will is revealed.

示す	しめす	to show
表示	ひょうじ	indication
… ◇ …		
公示	こうじ	public announcement
明示	めいじ	clear statement

89 村	village むら、ソン	一 十 才 木 木 村 村

Village 村 combines tree 木 and rule 寸, suggesting a place with trees where people live following the same rules.

村	むら	village
川村	かわむら	Kawamura (family name)
村長	そんちょう	village mayor
… ◇ …		
村人	むらびと	villager
村民	そんみん	villager

90 転	roll, turn テン	一	亠	丆	戸	百	亘	車	車
		転	転	転					

Wheels 車 make a sound, or "speak" 云 while rolling along.

自転車	じてんしゃ	bicycle
運転する	うんてんする	to drive
運転手	うんてんしゅ	driver
	… ◇ …	
転居する	てんきょする	to change one's residence
転校する	てんこうする	to change to another school

91 現	appear ゲン	一	丁	干	王	尹	珇	玥	玥
		玥	玥	現					

The king 王 emerged so the people can see 見 him.

現在地	げんざいち	place where one is now
現在	げんざい	the present, now
現住所	げんじゅうしょ	present address
	… ◇ …	
現代	げんだい	present age
現場	げんば	actual spot, such as a job site; field

4 PRACTICE

I. Write the readings of the following kanji in hiragana.

1. 小 学 校　　　2. 保 育 園　　　3. 自 転 車　　　4. 現 在 地

5. 表 示　　　6. 駐 車 場

7. 私の町は、人口が約 30 万人です。

8. 私立の高校に通っています。

9. むかし、日本人は、石で道具をつくりました。

10. この村には、大きい川があります。

11. 公園で、花や木を育てましょう。

Ⅱ. Fill in the blanks with appropriate kanji.

1. いく
教 □
education

2. むら
□
village

3. まち
□
town

4. こう
学 □
school

5. てん
自 □ 車
bicycle

6. ちゅう
□ 車場
parking lot

7. わたし
□
I

8. いし
□
stone

9. えん
動物 □
zoo

10. そだ
□ てる
to raise

11. げん
□ 住所
present address

12. かわ
□
river

5 SUPPLEMENT

Signs in Your Neighborhood

自転車置場
じてんしゃおきば
Bicycle Parking

広域避難所
こういきひなんじょ
Evacuation Area

駐車場歩行者入口
ちゅうしゃじょう ほこうしゃ いりぐち
Pedestrian Entrance to Parking

この食品の材料はなんですか

How to Read Food Labels

VENDORS ARE required to display the ingredients, date of production, expiration date, refrigeration instructions, and any other useful information on the label of all packaged food products. Ingredient labels are very important to people who have special diets. It is also a good idea to be cautious and check the expiration date, which is usually printed on the side or the bottom of the package. If you notice something wrong with a product, it is possible to get a refund by sending the package back to the manufacturer with a note about where and when it was purchased.

1 INTRODUCTORY QUIZ

Look at the illustrations below and refer to the words in VOCABULARY. Then try the following quiz.

Which label corresponds to each description below? Fill in the spaces with the correct letters (a～d) of the items.

1. 植物性油脂を使っているものはどれですか。　　　　(　　)(　　)

2. 添加物のない食物は、どれですか。　　　　　　　　(　　)(　　)(　　)

3. れいぞうこに入れなければならないものは、どれですか。(　　)(　　)

4. 賞味期間の一番ながいものはどれですか。　　　　　(　　)

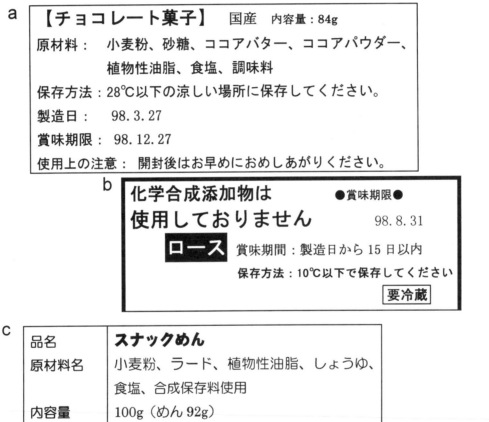

a 　【チョコレート菓子】　　国産　　内容量：84g

原材料：　小麦粉、砂糖、ココアバター、ココアパウダー、
　　　　　植物性油脂、食塩、調味料

保存方法：28℃以下の涼しい場所に保存してください。

製造日：　98.3.27

賞味期限：　98.12.27

使用上の注意：　開封後はお早めにおめしあがりください。

b 化学合成添加物は　　　　●賞味期限●
使用しておりません　　　　98.8.31

ロース　賞味期間：製造日から15日以内

保存方法：10℃以下で保存してください

要冷蔵

c 品名　　　スナックめん

原材料名　小麦粉、ラード、植物性油脂、しょうゆ、
　　　　　食塩、合成保存料使用

内容量　　100g（めん92g）

製造年月日　外側フィルムに表示

賞味期間　製造年月日より6ヶ月

保存方法　直射日光をさけ、常温保存

d 　　プロセスチーズ　　要冷蔵

●使用原料——ナチュラルチーズ

●内容量——95g

●保存上の注意——5℃前後で保存してください

●賞味期間——製造後8ヶ月（冷蔵保存）

2 VOCABULARY

Study the readings and meanings of these words to help you understand the INTRODUCTORY QUIZ.

1.	品名	ひん めい	name of product
2.	原材料	げん ざい りょう	raw material
3.	内容量	ない よう りょう	content volume
4.	植物性油脂	しょく ぶつ せい ゆ し	vegetable oil
5.	食塩	しょく えん	salt
6.	調味料	ちょう み りょう	seasoning
7.	賞味期限	しょう み き げん	expiration date
8.	賞味期間	しょう み き かん	expiration date
9.	製造年月日	せい ぞう ねん がっ ぴ	date of production
10.	保存方法	ほ ぞん ほう ほう	method of storage
11.	要冷蔵	よう れい ぞう	should be refrigerated
12.	化学合成	か がく ごう せい	synthetic substance
13.	添加物	てん か ぶつ	food additive
14.	合成保存料	ごう せい ほ ぞん りょう	synthetic preservative
15.	使用上の注意	し よう じょう の ちゅう い	use with caution
16.	保存上の注意	ほ ぞん じょう の ちゅう い	how to keep fresh

3 NEW CHARACTERS

Fifteen characters are introduced in this lesson. Use the explanations to help you understand and remember the characters. Study the compound words to increase your vocabulary.

原 材 植 油 脂 調 味 賞 限 製 存 要 蔵
添 加

92 原

original; field

はら、（ばら）、ゲン

一 厂 厂 厈 厉 盾 盾 原 原 原

Remember a spring 泉 running below a cliff 厂. A spring is the origin of water, thus 原 means by extension origin or wild field.

原宿	はらじゅく	Harajuku (place name)
秋葉原	あきはばら	Akihabara (place name)

… ◇ …

原始人	げんしじん	primitive man
原子	げんし	atom
原子力	げんしりょく	atomic energy
原理	げんり	theory

93 材

wood; material

ザイ

一 十 才 木 木 村 材

才, with the meaning to cut, and tree 木 combined, 材 means lumber.

原材料	げんざいりょう	ingredient

… ◇ …

人材	じんざい	human resource
題材	だいざい	subject matter
材木	ざいもく	lumber, timber

94 植

plant

う・える、ショク

一 十 才 木 木 朩 朾 柘 柏 栢 植 植

Plus 十, eye 目, and conceal ∟ together, 直 means to see straight. Most plants grow straight toward the sun. Thus 植 means plant.

植える	うえる	to plant
植物	しょくぶつ	plant

… ◇ …

植木	うえき	garden plant
植民地	しょくみんち	colony
田植え	たうえ	rice planting

95 油	oil あぶら、ユ	丶	ⅈ	シ	汋	沪	沖	油	油

由 is the pictograph of a bottle with a spout to pour liquid. Thus 由 means "something comes out of it." Oil is a liquid taken from the ground. Thus 油 means oil. Imagine a derrick. (cf. draw 抽, sleeve 袖, flute 笛)

油	あぶら	oil
植物油	しょくぶつゆ	vegetable oil
石油	せきゆ	petroleum
油性	ゆせい	oil-based

… ◇ …

96 脂	fat あぶら、シ	丿	刀	月	月	月′	肑	脂	脂
		脂	脂						

Meat 月 and tasty 旨 combined form this kanji.

脂	あぶら	oil
植物性油脂	しょくぶつせいゆし	vegetable oil
動物性油脂	どうぶつせいゆし	animal fat

… ◇ …

97 調	investigate, check; arrange しら・べる、チョウ	丶	亠	三	言	言	言	訂
		訓	訊	調	調	調	調	調

周 is the pictograph of a field full of rice plants. Together with 言, 調 means to ask and examine fully.

調べる	しらべる	to check

… ◇ …

調子	ちょうし	condition
調和する	ちょうわする	to harmonize
好調な	こうちょうな	in good condition

98 味	taste あじ、ミ	丿	冂	口	口⁻	口二	吁	吁	味

未 is the figure of top twigs not fully grown. Thus the potential is unknown. The combination of mouth 口 and unknown 未 means taste. Everyone likes to try the taste of the unknown.

味	あじ	taste
調味料	ちょうみりょう	seasoning
意味	いみ	meaning
	… ◇ …	
正味	しょうみ	net weight
中味	なかみ	contents

---

99 賞	prize; raise ショウ	丨	⸍	⺌	⺍⸌	产	尚	尚	当
		尚	尚	尚	賞	賞	賞	賞	

尚 depicts long wisps of smoke coming out of the chimney of a house. Combined with money 貝, 賞 means a plenty of money as a reward.

賞味する	しょうみする	to relish
ノーベル賞	ノーベルしょう	Nobel Prize
賞品	しょうひん	prize
賞金	しょうきん	prize money
	… ◇ …	
受賞者	じゅしょうしゃ	prize winner

---

100 限	limit ゲン	⁊	⁊	ß	ß⁻	ßヲ	ßヨ	阝	限
		限							

艮 means to stop and stare. Stone wall 阝 is added to mean a boundary. By extension, it means limit.

期限	きげん	time limit
無限	むげん	infinite
	… ◇ …	
限度	げんど	limit
門限	もんげん	curfew
制限速度	せいげんそくど	speed limit

101 製	produce, manufacture セイ	ノ	⺊	⺹	牛	牲	制	制	制
		制	制	製	製	製	製		

牜 represents many trees and when combined with knife リ, 制 meant to make something out of wood using a knife. 衣 is the pictograph of clothing. Three elements combined, 製 meant to make clothing and now means to make things in general.	製造	せいぞう	manufacture
	日本製	にほんせい	made in Japan
	製品	せいひん	product
	… ◇ …		
	製法	せいほう	manufacturing method

102 存	exist ソン、ゾン	一	ナ	才	存	存	存		

Talent 才 exists 存 in a child 子.	保存する	ほぞんする	to preserve
	… ◇ …		
	存在	そんざい	existence
	生存	せいぞん	existence, life
	共存	きょうぞん	coexistence

103 要	main point; necessity, need ヨウ	一	厂	戸	襾	襾	西	要	要
		要							

Traditionally a woman's 女 waist was a central physical feature and by extension 要 has come to mean important.	要	よう	necessary to
	不要な	ふような	not necessary
	… ◇ …		
	重要な	じゅうような	important
	主要な	しゅような	main
	所要時間	しょようじかん	required time

104 蔵	storehouse くら、ゾウ	一	十	艹	疒	产	产	芹	芹
		芹	芹	芹	蓙	蔵	蔵	蔵	

臧 means oblong. Combined with plant 艹, 蔵 refers to an oblong building in which to store the harvest. Thus it means a storehouse.

蔵	くら	storehouse
冷蔵庫	れいぞうこ	refrigerator
要冷蔵	ようれいぞう	keep refrigerated
	… ◇ …	
蔵書	ぞうしょ	collection of books

105 添	add; accompany そ・える、テン	ヽ	ミ	シ	ジ	沙	汙	沃	添
		添	添	添					

Heaven 天 and heart 心 combined, 忝 means a flat thing sticking to something. Adding water 氵, 添 means to add.

添える	そえる	to add to
	… ◇ …	

106 加	add; join カ	フ	カ	加	加	加			

Physical power 力 and the power of speech 口 combine to mean to add.

添加物	てんかぶつ	additive
加入する	かにゅうする	to be a member
	… ◇ …	
加工品	かこうひん	processed food
参加する	さんかする	to take part in, to attend

4 PRACTICE

Ⅰ. Write the readings of the following kanji in hiragana.

1. 原 材 料   2. 植 物   3. 油 脂   4. 無 限

5. 調 味 料   6. 要 冷 蔵   7. 添 加 物

8. 日本製の車を買いました。

9. 賞味期限は、5月8日です。

10. 10度以下で、保存してください。

11. プラスチックは、石油製品です。

12. 山に、花や木を植えましょう。

13. これは、日本人が好きな味です。

Ⅱ. Fill in the blanks with appropriate kanji.

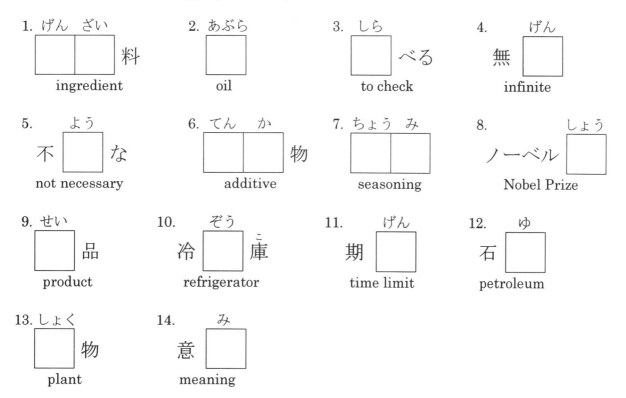

1. げん ざい
　□□料
　ingredient

2. あぶら
　□
　oil

3. しら
　□べる
　to check

4. げん
　無□
　infinite

5. よう
　不□な
　not necessary

6. てん か
　□□物
　additive

7. ちょう み
　□□
　seasoning

8. しょう
　ノーベル□
　Nobel Prize

9. せい
　□品
　product

10. ぞう こ
　冷□庫
　refrigerator

11. げん
　期□
　time limit

12. ゆ
　石□
　petroleum

13. しょく
　□物
　plant

14. み
　意□
　meaning

REVIEW EXERCISE Lessons 1－9

I . Find kanji having common radicals and write them or the corresponding letters in the blanks.

木 1. (　　　) 2. (　　　) 3. (　　　) 4. (　　　) 5. (　　　)

氵 6. (　　　) 7. (　　　) 8. (　　　) 9. (　　　) 10. (　　　)

宀 11. (　　　) 12. (　　　) 13. (　　　)

彳 14. (　　　) 15. (　　　) 16. (　　　)

> a. 村　　b. 油　　c. 宅　　d. 植　　e. 待　　f. 材
> g. 港　　h. 枚　　i. 客　　j. 役　　k. 活　　l. 校
> m. 得　　n. 酒　　o. 家　　p. 添

II . Fill in the blanks with appropriate kanji or the corresponding letters from the list below.

1. 家 (　　　) rent

2. (　　　) 家 vacant house

3. 税 (　　　) tax

4. 税 (　　　) customs

5. (　　　) 税 duty-free

6. 旅 (　　　) trip

7. 旅 (　　　) traveler

8. 旅 (　　　) inn

9. (　　　) 理 cooking

10. (　　　) 理 management

11. 建 (　　　) building

12. 一 (　　　) 建 house

13. 二 (　　　) 建 two-story

14. (　　　) 園 park

15. 保 (　　　) 園 day nursery

> a. 保　　b. 育　　c. 空　　d. 免　　e. 行　　f. 金　　g. 一
> h. 戸　　i. 客　　j. 物　　k. 公　　l. 料　　m. 賃　　n. 消
> o. 費　　p. 二　　q. 階　　r. 関　　s. 館　　t. 管

どの洗剤を使いますか

Cleansers for the Kitchen and Clothing

IN JAPAN, there are many kinds of household cleaning products. These are usually divided into items that are safe to use around food (kitchen cleansers) and items that are not (detergents). Of the latter, there are two kinds: one for cotton and synthetic fibers, and the other for wool, silk, and delicate fabrics. For safety's sake, it is important to differentiate between cleaning products. In this lesson you will learn the words on containers of household cleaning agents.

1 INTRODUCTORY QUIZ

Look at the illustrations below and refer to the words in VOCABULARY. Then try the following quiz.

These are labels and instructions about how to use the detergents and bleaches below.

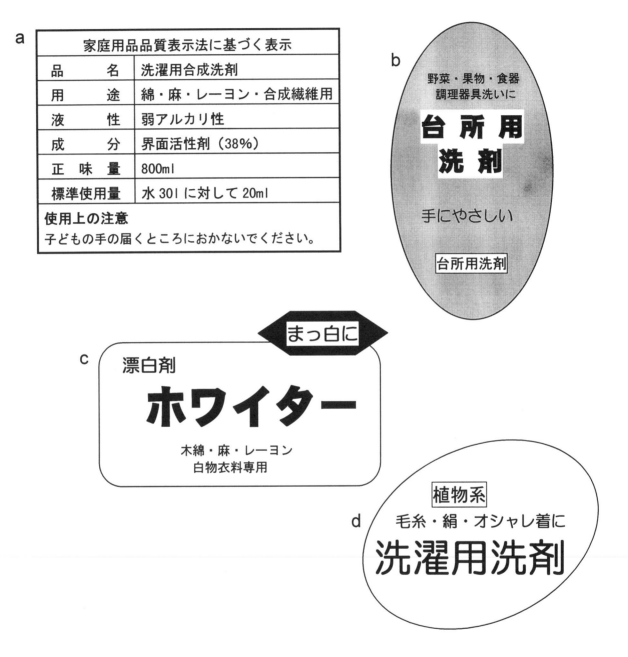

a

家庭用品品質表示法に基づく表示	
品　　　名	洗濯用合成洗剤
用　　　途	綿・麻・レーヨン・合成繊維用
液　　　性	弱アルカリ性
成　　　分	界面活性剤（38%）
正　味　量	800ml
標準使用量	水 30l に対して 20ml

使用上の注意
子どもの手の届くところにおかないでください。

b

野菜・果物・食器
調理器具洗いに

台所用
洗剤

手にやさしい

台所用洗剤

c

まっ白に

漂白剤

ホワイター

木綿・麻・レーヨン
白物衣料専用

d

植物系

毛糸・絹・オシャレ着に

洗濯用洗剤

Which cleanser or bleach (above) is appropriate for each of the items listed below? Fill in the spaces with the correct letters (a～d).

1. もめんの T シャツを洗う　　（　　　　　）　　2. タオルを白くする　　　　　（　　　　　）

3. 食器を洗う　　　　　　　　（　　　　　）　　4. 野菜を洗う　　　　　　　　（　　　　　）

5. レーヨンのシャツを白くする（　　　　　）　　6. ウールのセーターを洗う　　（　　　　　）

2 VOCABULARY

Study the readings and meanings of these words to help you understand the INTRODUC-TORY QUIZ.

1. 衣料 　　　　　　 い りょう 　　　　　　 clothing
2. 洗剤 　　　　　　 せん ざい 　　　　　　 detergent
3. 家庭用品 　　　　 か てい よう ひん 　　 home furnishing
4. 品質表示 　　　　 ひん しつ ひょう じ 　 indication of quality
5. 品名 　　　　　　 ひん めい 　　　　　　 name of article/item
6. 用途 　　　　　　 よう と 　　　　　　　 use
7. 液性 　　　　　　 えき せい 　　　　　　 nature of liquid
8. 成分 　　　　　　 せい ぶん 　　　　　　 ingredient
9. 合成洗剤 　　　　 ごう せい せん ざい 　 synthetic cleanser
10. 洗濯用 　　　　　 せん たく よう 　　　 for laundry
11. 台所用 　　　　　 だい どころ よう 　　 for kitchen
12. 植物系 　　　　　 しょく ぶつ けい 　　 vegetable matter
13. 綿 　　　　　　　 めん 　　　　　　　　 cotton
14. 麻 　　　　　　　 あさ 　　　　　　　　 hemp
15. レーヨン 　　　　　　　　　　　　　　　 rayon
16. 毛 　　　　　　　 け 　　　　　　　　　 wool
17. 絹 　　　　　　　 きぬ 　　　　　　　　 silk
18. 漂白剤 　　　　　 ひょう はく ざい 　　 bleach
19. 白物衣料 　　　　 しろ もの い りょう 　 white clothing
20. 野菜 　　　　　　 や さい 　　　　　　　 vegetable
21. 果物 　　　　　　 くだ もの 　　　　　　 fruit
22. 食器 　　　　　　 しょっ き 　　　　　　 tableware
23. 調理器具 　　　　 ちょう り き ぐ 　　　 kitchen utensil

3 NEW CHARACTERS

Eleven characters are introduced in this lesson. Use the explanations to help you understand and remember the characters. Study the compound words to increase your vocabulary.

衣 台 剤 庭 質 綿 毛 白 野 菜 果

107 衣	clothing ころも、イ	`	一	ナ	ナ	衣	衣		

衣 derives from the pictograph of the kimono's V-shaped neckline.

衣類	いるい	clothing
	… ◇ …	
衣服	いふく	clothes
衣	ころも	clothes

108 台	table; pedestal; counter for cars and machines ダイ、タイ	ム	ム	台	台	台			

There are many things ム to eat 口 on the table.

台	だい	table
台所	だいどころ	kitchen
車が三台	くるまがさんだい	three cars
	… ◇ …	
土台	どだい	foundation

109 剤	medicine; dose ザイ	`	一	ナ	文	文	斉	斉	斉
		斉	剤						

斉 means equal. Chinese medicinal herbs are cut into portions, or doses, with a knife 刂.

洗剤	せんざい	detergent
	… ◇ …	
薬剤	やくざい	medicine
調剤薬局	ちょうざいやっきょく	prescription pharmacy

110 庭 yard

にわ、テイ

| ` | 亠 | 广 | 广 | 广 | 庐 | 庭 | 庭 |
| 庭 | 庭 | | | | | | |

廷 means to spread and 广 means a house. Thus 庭 means a flat place in the estate, or yard.

庭	にわ	garden
家庭	かてい	home
	… ◇ …	
庭園	ていえん	garden
校庭	こうてい	schoolyard

111 質 quality; nature

シツ

| ノ | ィ | ┌ | 斤 | 斤' | 竹' | 斤斤 | 竹竹 |
| 竹 | 竹 | 笪 | 質 | 質 | 質 | 質 | |

Two hacksaws 竹 above a shell 貝 like an oyster are ready to cut it open to find out the quality of the pearl inside it. Thus 質 means quality.

品質	ひんしつ	quality
性質	せいしつ	nature, property
	… ◇ …	
質問	しつもん	question
物質	ぶっしつ	material, substance
本質	ほんしつ	essence, substance

112 綿 cotton

わた、メン

| く | 乡 | 幺 | 乡 | 糸 | 糸' | 糸l |
| 紀 | 綿 | 綿 | 綿 | 綿 | 綿 | |

White 白, cloth 巾, and thread 糸 combined, 綿 is the thread for making white cloth.

綿	めん	cotton
綿	わた	(raw) cotton
木綿	もめん	cotton
	… ◇ …	
海綿	かいめん	sponge

113	wool	ノ	⺵	乍	毛				
毛	け、（げ）、モウ								

毛 is the pictograph of hair or fur.

毛	け	wool
	… ◇ …	
まゆ毛	まゆげ	eyebrow
原毛	げんもう	raw wool
不毛	ふもう	barren, sterile

114	white	ノ	亻	白	白	白			
白	しろ・い、ハク								

白 is a simplified form of white rice.

白い	しろい	white
白線	はくせん	white line
白紙	はくし	blank paper
白人	はくじん	Caucasian
	… ◇ …	
空白	くうはく	blank
白書	はくしょ	white paper (official paper)
自白	じはく	confession

115	field, plain; wild	㇆	口	日	甲	甲	里	里乛	里マ
野	の、ヤ	野乛	野						

Village 里 and previous 予 combine to mean 野, a previous state of the village, or a wild field.

野原	のはら	field, plain
平野	へいや	a plain; Hirano (family name)
	… ◇ …	
野生	やせい	wild (animal, plant)
分野	ぶんや	field (of endeavor)

116	
菜	vegetable
	サイ

一	十	ナ	ナ	ヤ	ヤ	ヤ	芒
苂	苹	菜					

To the pictographs for hand ⍦ and plants ⺾, tree 木 is added to mean the picked plant.

野菜	やさい	vegetable
菜食の	さいしょくの	vegetarian
	… ◇ …	
菜園	さいえん	vegetable garden
山菜	さんさい	edible wild plant

117	
果	fruit; result
	カ

丨	冂	戸	日	旦	甲	里	果

This is the pictograph of a tree bearing fruit.

果物	*くだもの	fruit
	… ◇ …	
結果	けっか	result
成果	せいか	result

4 PRACTICE

Ⅰ. Write the readings of the following kanji in hiragana.

1. 衣 類   2. 台 所   3. 洗 剤   4. 家 庭   5. 品 質

6. 綿 シャツ   7. 白 い   8. 野 菜   9. 果 物

10. 私の家の庭に、花を植えました。

11. この上着は、毛 100％です。

12. 車が、三台止まっています。

13. 歯をみがいて、白くしましょう。

II. Fill in the blanks with appropriate kanji.

1. や　さい
□□
vegetable

2. くだ
□ 物
fruit

3. しろ
□ い
white

4. ざい
洗 □
detergent

5. い
□ 類
clothes

6. け
□
wool

7. めん
□
cotton

8. しつ
品 □
quality

9. にわ
□
garden

10. だい
□ 所
kitchen

11. てい
家 □
home

5 SUPPLEMENT

Instructions for washing, drying, and ironing

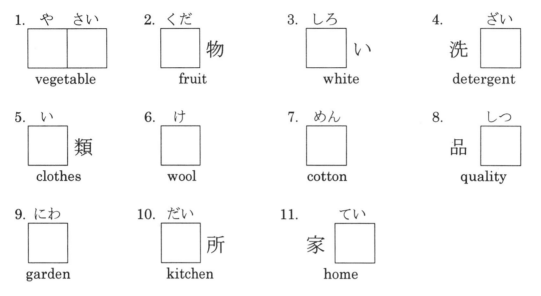

hand wash medium 30℃　　do not hand wash　　machine wash　　delicate warm wash

dry clean only　　do not dry clean　　iron medium　　do not iron　　dry in shade

ルーム エアコンの使い方

How to Use a Room-Temperature Remote Control

THANKS TO technological development, Japanese houses are full of electrical appliances. New models are produced every year. There are many stores that stock only electrical and electronic appliances: Akihabara is a Tokyo district famous for such specialized stores. To use the products, you will need to read manuals, some of which are written only in Japanese. In this lesson, you will learn how to use the room-temperature remote control when the function buttons are labeled in kanji.

1 | INTRODUCTORY QUIZ

Look at the illustration below and refer to the words in VOCABULARY. Then try the following quiz.

Which button will you push when you want to do the following? Write the correct letters (a～i) in the spaces provided.

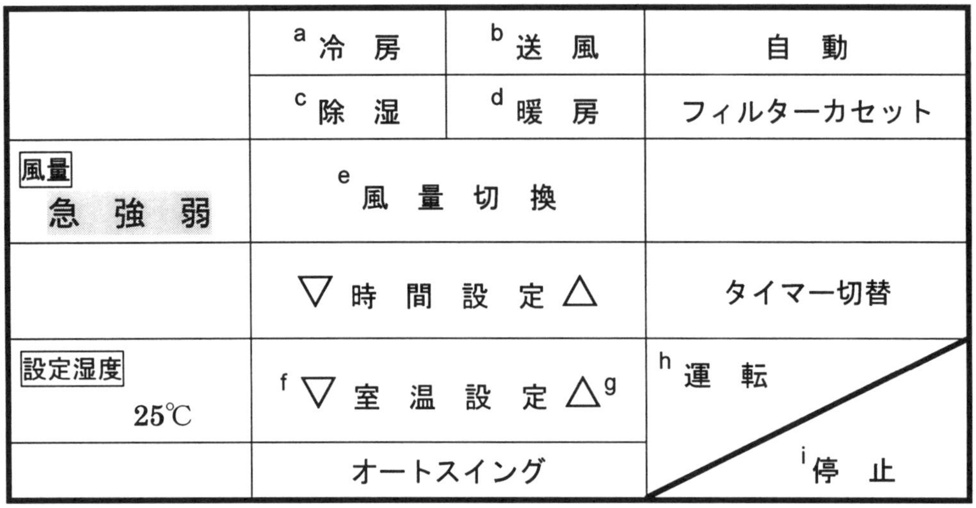

		a 冷　房	b 送　風	自　動
		c 除　湿	d 暖　房	フィルターカセット
風量 急　強　弱		e 風　量　切　換		
		▽　時　間　設　定　△		タイマー切替
設定湿度 　　25℃		f ▽　室　温　設　定　△g		h 運　転
		オートスイング		i 停　止

1. エアコンをつける　　　　　（　　　　）
2. エアコンをとめる　　　　　（　　　　）
3. 冷房にする　　　　　　　　（　　　　）
4. 暖房にする　　　　　　　　（　　　　）
5. へやの温度を下げる　　　　（　　　　）
6. へやの温度を上げる　　　　（　　　　）
7. 風量を切り換える　　　　　（　　　　）

2 | VOCABULARY

Study the readings and meanings of these words to help you understand the INTRODUCTORY QUIZ.

1. 冷房　　　れい　ぼう　　　　air conditioning
2. 暖房　　　だん　ぼう　　　　heating
3. 除湿　　　じょ　しつ　　　　dry
4. 運転　　　うん　てん　　　　power on
5. 停止　　　てい　し　　　　　power off

6.	室温設定	しつ おん せっ てい	temperature setting
7.	風量切換[13]	ふう りょう きり かえ	fan speed
8.	自動	じ どう	automatic
9.	送風[5]	そう ふう	fan
10.	強	きょう	strong
11.	弱	じゃく	light/weak
12.	急	きゅう	rapid

3 NEW CHARACTERS

Ten characters are introduced in this lesson. Use the explanations to help you understand and remember the characters. Study the compound words to increase your vocabulary.

暖 房 運 温 設 風 強 弱 度 量

118 暖	warm あたた・かい、ダン	丨 冂 月 日 日´ 日＜ 日＜ 日˙˙ 日丷 日ᵒ 日ᵒ 日ᵒ 暖

爰 depicts two hands, and the sun 日 shining on them brings warmth.	暖かい	あたたかい	warm
		… ◇ …	
	暖冬	だんとう	warm winter
	暖流	だんりゅう	warm current

119 房	room; wife ボウ	一	ラ	ヨ	戸	戸	戸	房	房

戸 means door, or partition, and 方 means side. 房 is a little room partitioned off from a larger room. Originally a wife remained in the smaller room.	暖房	だんぼう	heating
	冷房	れいぼう	air conditioning
		… ◇ …	
	女房	にょうぼう	one's own wife

120 運	carry, transport; fate, luck はこ・ぶ、ウン	ノ	⼾	⼾	尸	目	目	冒	宣
		軍	軍	運	運				

軍, a combination of roof ⼍ and vehicle 車, means armed forces. Imagine tanks used for battle. To go ⻌ is added to mean to carry. By extension, 運 also means luck, because luck is a vehicle that carries a person along without the person's efforts or initiative.	運ぶ	はこぶ	to carry
	運転する	うんてんする	to drive
	運転手	うんてんしゅ	driver
	運動する	うんどうする	to move; to campaign
	運	うん	luck
		… ◇ …	
	不運な	ふうんな	unlucky

121 温	warm あたた・かい、オン	丶	⼆	シ	シ	沪	沪	沪	沪
		渇	浘	浘	温				

Sunshine 日 makes the water ⺡ in a dish 皿 warm. Thus 温 means warm.	温かい	あたたかい	warm
	室温	しつおん	room temperature
	温度	おんど	temperature
	気温	きおん	air temperature
	体温	たいおん	body temperature
	体温計	たいおんけい	clinical thermometer
		… ◇ …	
	温室	おんしつ	greenhouse

122 設	establish, set up セツ、（セッ）	丶	亠	亠	言	言	言	言	言
		訁	設	設					

Speech 言 and a symbol of an action 殳 combined, 設 means to establish.

設定する	せっていする	to set up
設備	せつび	facility
	… ◇ …	
建設する	けんせつする	to construct
設計する	せっけいする	to design
設立する	せつりつする	to establish

123 風	wind; appearance; style かぜ、フウ	ノ	几	几	凡	凮	凮	風
		風						

A sail 几 and a worm 虫 coming out from the ground 一 in spring when spring winds start blowing. Combined, 風 means wind.

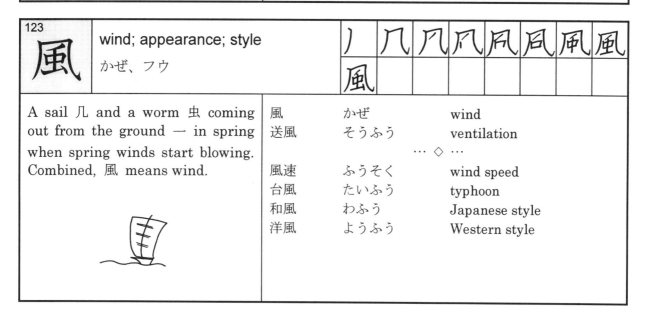

風	かぜ	wind
送風	そうふう	ventilation
	… ◇ …	
風速	ふうそく	wind speed
台風	たいふう	typhoon
和風	わふう	Japanese style
洋風	ようふう	Western style

124 強	strong つよ・い、キョウ	フ	コ	弓	弓	弘	弘	弨
		強	強	強				

弓 means a strong bow. Katakana ム and a worm 虫 suggest a strong insect. Together they refer to a strong hard insect, like a beetle. Now this kanji means strong.

強い	つよい	strong
強風	きょうふう	strong wind
	… ◇ …	
強力	きょうりょく	strength
強気	つよき	bullish

125 弱	weak よわ・い、ジャク	フ	コ	弓	弓	弓	弓ˊ	弓ˊ	弱
		弱	弱						

弱 means a decorative bow not as strong as an ordinary bow. Therefore, 弱 means weak.	弱い	よわい	weak
	弱風	じゃくふう	weak wind
		… ◇ …	
	弱気	よわき	faintheartedness
	弱者	じゃくしゃ	the disadvantaged

126 度	degree; limit; times ド	'	亠	广	广	庐	庐	庐	度
		度							

Hand 又 combined with 庐 means to measure by hand. In ancient China, people measured objects using their hands. Thus 度 means degree.	温度	おんど	temperature
		… ◇ …	
	今度	こんど	this time; next time
	毎度	まいど	every time
	速度	そくど	speed
	制度	せいど	system

127 量	quantity リョウ	丶	冂	厃	日	旦	昌	昌	昌
		昌	昌	畳	量				

Day 日 and heavy 重 combined, 量 means quantity.	風量	ふうりょう	wind volume
		… ◇ …	
	音量	おんりょう	volume
	重量	じゅうりょう	weight
	分量	ぶんりょう	amount
	大量の	たいりょうの	a lot of

4 PRACTICE

I. Write the readings of the following kanji in hiragana.

1. 暖 房   2. 冷 房   3. 運 転   4. 室 温   5. 設 定

6. 強 風   7. 弱 風

8. 今日は、風が弱いです。

9. 気温は、25度です。

10. 体を強くするために、毎日、運動しています。

11. この建物は、設備がいいです。

12. 南向きの部屋は、暖かいです。

13. この荷物を、車で運んでください。

14. 水の量は、これでいいですか。

II. Fill in the blanks with appropriate kanji.

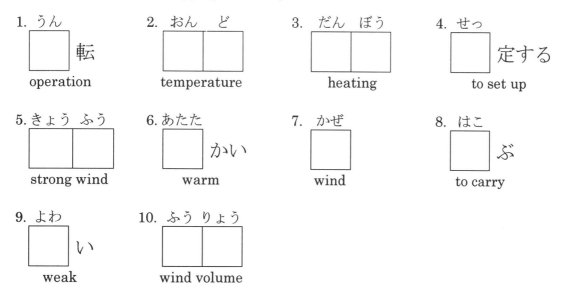

1. うん
□ 転
operation

2. おん　ど
□□
temperature

3. だん　ぼう
□□
heating

4. せっ
□ 定する
to set up

5. きょう　ふう
□□
strong wind

6. あたた
□ かい
warm

7. かぜ
□
wind

8. はこ
□ ぶ
to carry

9. よわ
□ い
weak

10. ふう　りょう
□□
wind volume

Rice Cookers　炊飯器

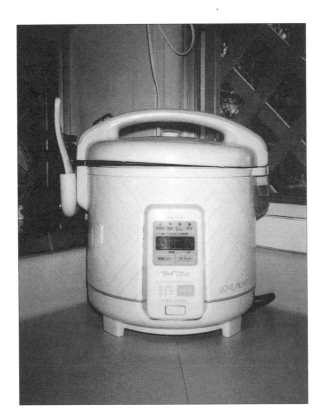

炊飯器 すいはんき	rice cooker
余熱炊き よねつだ	pre-cook
炊飯 すいはん	start
保温 ほおん	keep warm
時間セット じかん	hour set
分セット ふん	minute set
電源　入／切 でんげん　いり　きり	power on/off

Electric Thermal Pots　電気温水ポット

電気温水ポット でんきおんすい	electric thermal pot
止める と	stop
出す だ	pour
満水 まんすい	full tank
給水 きゅうすい	water supply
沸かす わ	boil
保温 ほおん	keep warm

ビデオの使い方

Using a VCR

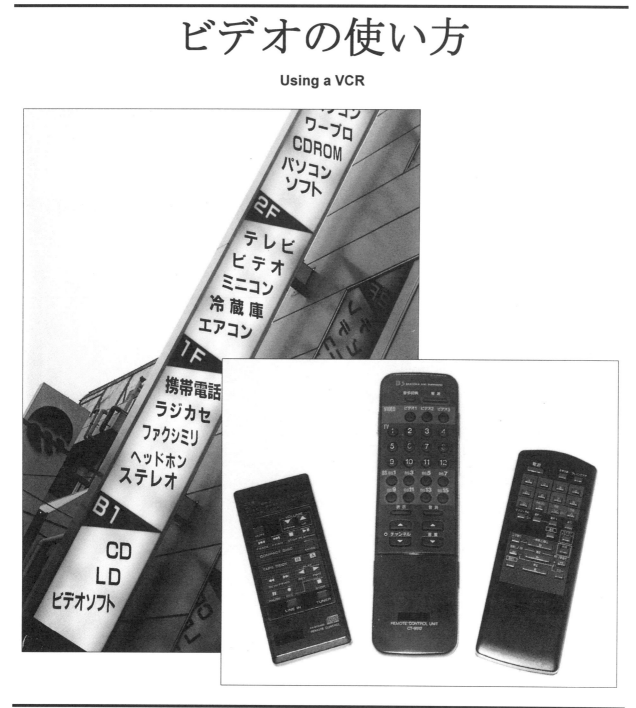

NOWADAYS, THERE are few Japanese homes without a VCR. By recording their favorite shows on video or renting videos from a neighborhood shop, people can enjoy their favorite dramas, sports events, music performances, or classic movies anytime they want to. VCRs have come to be an important part of home entertainment. In this lesson, you will study the kanji written on the video machine, so that you can record or play videotapes without difficulty.

1 INTRODUCTORY QUIZ

Look at the illustration below and refer to the words in VOCABULARY. Then try the following quiz.

Ⅰ. Here is a user's manual for a video cassette recorder. You will learn how to play or record a tape by reading the manual.

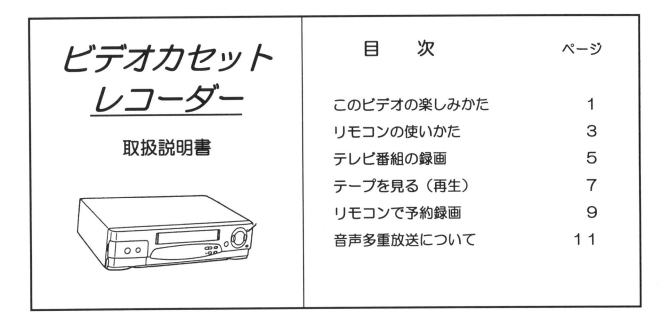

ビデオカセット
レコーダー

取扱説明書

目　　次	ページ
このビデオの楽しみかた	1
リモコンの使いかた	3
テレビ番組の録画	5
テープを見る（再生）	7
リモコンで予約録画	9
音声多重放送について	11

Which button will you push when you want to do the following? Write the correct letter (a〜h) in the spaces provided.

a. 音量　volume

b. 巻き戻し　rewind

c. 電源　switch

d. 録画　videotape

e. 早送り　fast forward

f. 再生　play

g. 停止　stop

h. 一時停止　pause

Example　巻き戻す　　　（　b　）
1. 録画する　　　　　（　　）
2. スイッチを入れる　（　　）
3. ビデオを見る　　　（　　）
4. 音を大きくする　　（　　）
5. 早く送る　　　　　（　　）
6. 止める　　　　　　（　　）
7. ちょっととめる　　（　　）

2   VOCABULARY

Study the readings and meanings of these words to help you understand the INTRODUC-
TORY QUIZ.

1.	取扱説明書	とり あつかい せつ めい しょ	manual
2.	目次	もく じ	table of contents
3.	音声多重	おん せい た じゅう	multiplex
4.	再生	さい せい	play
5.	録画	ろく が	videotape recording
6.	電源	でん げん	switch
7.	一時停止	いち じ てい し	pause
8.	巻戻し	まき もど し	rewind
9.	早送り	はや おく り	fast forward
10.	音量	おん りょう	volume

3   NEW CHARACTERS

Ten characters are introduced in this lesson. Use the explanations to help you understand
and remember the characters. Study the compound words to increase your vocabulary.

説 次 音 声 多 重 再 画 源 早

128 説	opinion, theory; explain セツ							

A person with a big mouth 口 is a big brother 兄 who gives advice to his siblings. The words 言 of an older brother 兄 with horns ゛are powerful and assertive. Thus 説 means to explain, persuade, or preach a doctrine.	説明書	せつめいしょ	manual
	小説	しょうせつ	novel
		… ◇ …	
	ニュース解説	ニュースかいせつ	news commentary
	社説	しゃせつ	editorial
	学説	がくせつ	theory

129 次	next; the second つぎ、ジ	`	冫	ン	汀	浐	次		

欠 is the pictograph of a man yawning with his mouth wide open. 欠 combined with ice 冫 means next.

次	つぎ	next
目次	もくじ	table of contents
	… ◇ …	
次男	じなん	second son
二次	にじ	second

---

130 音	sound おと、オン、イン	`	立	广	亢	立	产	音	音
		音							

When a new day 日 arises 立, people begin to make sounds.

音	おと	sound
発音	はつおん	pronunciation
音読み	おんよみ	*on*-reading (of kanji)
	… ◇ …	
音楽会	おんがくかい	concert
母音	ぼいん	vowel
子音	しいん	consonant

---

131 声	voice こえ、（ごえ）、セイ	一	十	士	吉	吉	吉	声	

声 depicts a simple Chinese instrument (slate bars hanging on strings).

声	こえ	voice
音声	おんせい	sound
	… ◇ …	
大声で	おおごえで	in a loud voice
声楽家	せいがくか	vocalist

| 132 多 | many, much
おお・い、タ | ノ | ク | タ | 夕 | 多 | 多 | | |
| | | | | | | | | | |

With two evening 夕, 多 means that many days have passed and means in general many or much.	多い	おおい	many
	多分	たぶん	probably
		··· ◇ ···	
	多少	たしょう	a little
	多額の	たがくの	a large sum of (money)

| 133 重 | heavy
おも・い、ジュウ | ノ | ㇒ | 亻 | 台 | 台 | 台 | 重 | 重 |
| | | 重 | | | | | | | |

This is the figure of a man with a heavy pack on his back.	重い	おもい	heavy
	音声多重	おんせいたじゅう	multiplex
		··· ◇ ···	
	体重	たいじゅう	body weight
	重体	じゅうたい	serious illness
	重力	じゅうりょく	gravity
	重工業	じゅうこうぎょう	heavy industry

| 134 再 | once more, again, twice
サイ | 一 | 冂 | 冋 | 両 | 再 | 再 | | |
| | | | | | | | | | |

冉 is a simplified figure of a basket upside down. — is added to mean one more time, or again.	再生	さいせい	recycle, playback
	再発行する	さいはっこうする	to reissue
	再入国する	さいにゅうこくする	to reenter a country
		··· ◇ ···	
	再会する	さいかいする	to meet again
	再利用する	さいりようする	to recycle

135

画

draw, picture; stroke

ガ、カク

一 一 一 币 雨 面 画 画

画 meant to draw a boundary, 凵 and 一, around a rice paddy 田. Thus 画 means to draw.

録画する	ろくがする	to record
日本画	にほんが	Japanese-style painting
	… ◇ …	
漢字の画数	かんじのかくすう	kanji stroke count
画家	がか	artist, painter
計画する	けいかくする	to plan

136

源

source, origin

ゲン

丶 冫 氵 氵 氵 氵 氵 沂
沂 沪 源 源 源

原 is plain or original. Water 氵 is added to create the figurative sense of origin.

電源	でんげん	switch
	… ◇ …	
水源	すいげん	a riverhead

137

早

early, fast

はや・い、ソウ

丨 冂 冃 日 旦 早

The sun 日 is rising just above a field of plants 木 early in the morning.

早送り	はやおくり	fast forward
	… ◇ …	
早々に	そうそうに	early, immediate
早期発見	そうきはっけん	early detection
早めに	はやめに	a little early

4 PRACTICE

Ⅰ. Write the readings of the following kanji in hiragana.

1. 説 明 書　　　2. 目 次　　　　3. 音 声 多 重　　　4. 再 生

5. 録 画　　　　6. 音 声　　　7. 早 送 り

8. テレビの電源を切ってから、ねます。

9. 東京は、人も車も多いです。

10. 音を大きくしてください。

11. 次の日は、早くおきました。

12. 外で、こどもの声がします。

13. この荷物は、重いです。

Ⅱ. Fill in the blanks with appropriate kanji.

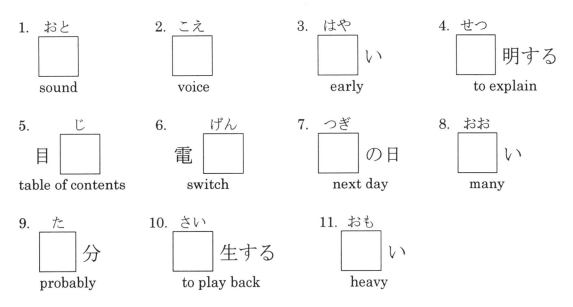

1. おと
□
sound

2. こえ
□
voice

3. はや
□ い
early

4. せつ
□ 明する
to explain

5. じ
目 □
table of contents

6. げん
電 □
switch

7. つぎ
□ の日
next day

8. おお
□ い
many

9. た
□ 分
probably

10. さい
□ 生する
to play back

11. おも
□ い
heavy

Telephone with Fax　ファックスつき電話

子機
remote
handset

A4サイズ

=送信も受信も前から！=

登録	enter number (speed dial)
停止	stop
転送	send
バッテリー電源	battery power
内線	extension
留守	message and play
保留	hold
通話予約	fax reservation

パソコンを使いましょう

Using a Personal Computer

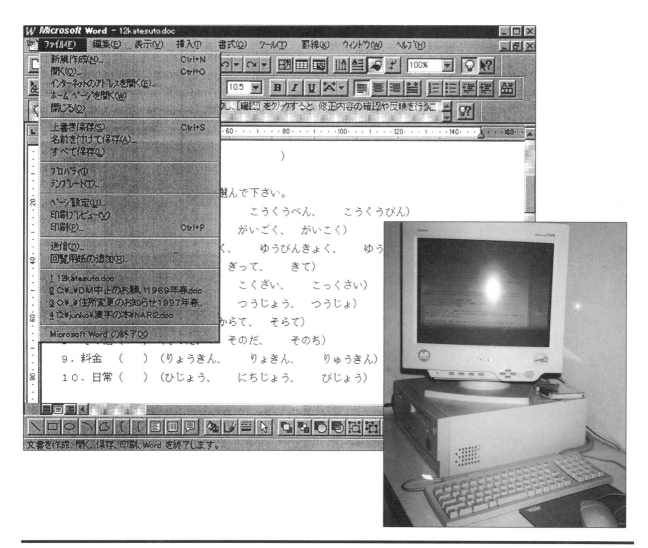

THIS IS the age of computers. Computers are used in offices, schools, shops, and homes. The sales of personal computers have soared in the past several years. People use personal computers for different purposes: for business, academic research, or entertainment. When you turn on the machine, many kanji words appear on the screen. To operate the computer and to get what you want in the dialogue box, you must know the technical terms for computer functions written in kanji on the screen. In this lesson, you will learn typical computer words for functions like edit (編集), create (新規作成), format (書式), print (印刷), delete (削除), and save (保存). Then you will know which key to push and which function on the menu bar to point to and click. That way, you can make the most use of your personal computer.

1 INTRODUCTORY QUIZ

Look at the illustration below and refer to the words in VOCABULARY. Then try the following quiz.

These words are often used in computers. Match the kanji word and its English meaning.

1. 編集 ( ) 2. 新規作成 ( ) 3. 印刷 ( ) 4. 終了 ( )
5. 選択 ( ) 6. 検索 ( ) 7. 置換 ( ) 8. 削除 ( )
9. 漢字 ( ) 10. 英数 ( )

a. replace	b. find	c. select	d. edit	e. create	f. kanji
g. quit	h. print	i. delete	j. English and number		

2 VOCABULARY

Study the readings and meanings of these words to help you understand the INTRODUCTORY QUIZ.

1. 編集 　　へん しゅう 　　edit
2. 新規作成 　　しん き さく せい 　　create
3. 印刷 　　いん さつ 　　print
4. 終了 　　しゅう りょう 　　quit
5. 選択 　　せん たく 　　select
6. 検索 　　けん さく 　　find
7. 置換 　　ち かん 　　replace
8. 削除 　　さく じょ 　　delete
9. 漢字 　　かん じ 　　kanji
10. 英数 　　えい すう 　　English and number

3 NEW CHARACTERS

Twelve characters are introduced in this lesson. Use the explanations to help you understand and remember the characters. Study the compound words to increase your vocabulary.

漢 英 編 規 削 除 印 刷 換 選 検 了

138 漢	Chinese; fellow カン	ヽ	ヽ	シ	シー	シナ	シナ	シナ	シナ
		汢	渲	漢	漢	漢			

People 夫 living in the green ⺾ area at the mouth 口 of a river or water 氵 founded the country of China.	漢字	かんじ	kanji
		… ◇ …	
	門外漢	もんがいかん	outsider, layman

139 英	brilliant, talented; English エイ	一	艹	ヤ	艹	艻	节	艻	英

Plant ⺾ and center 央 means an exceptionally beautiful flower. Thus 英 now means talented, or brave.	英数	えいすう	English and number
	英語	えいご	English
	英文	えいぶん	English sentence
	英会話	えいかいわ	English conversation
	英国	えいこく	England
		… ◇ …	

140 編	knit, crochet; compile, edit あ・む、ヘン	㇛	幺	幺	糸	糸	糸	糸	糸
		紀	紗	紗	絧	絹	編	編	

A woman is knitting 冊 with yarn 糸 by the door 戸.	編集する	へんしゅうする	to edit
	編集者	へんしゅうしゃ	editor
		… ◇ …	
	編む	あむ	to knit, to crochet

141 規 — rule, norm, standard

キ

Stroke order: 一　二　丰　夫　夫l　夫П　夫月　夫目　耟　耟　規

A man or husband 夫 observes 見 the rules 規 of society.

新規作成する	しんきさくせいする	to create
規則	きそく	rule

… ◇ …

142 削 — delete, cut down little by little

けず・る、サク

Stroke order: 丿　丷　⺌　⺍　肖　肖　肖　肖'　削

The size of a cut of meat 月 is gradually reduced 小 with a knife 刂.

削る	けずる	to sharpen (a pencil), to whittle, to pare
添削する	てんさくする	to correct

… ◇ …

143 除 — exclude

ジョ

Stroke order: 乛　了　阝　阝'　阝\　阾　阾　除　阶　除

The extra 余 field is fenced off, or excluded, by a stone wall 阝.

削除する	さくじょする	to delete

… ◇ …

除名する	じょめいする	to expel

144 印	press, print; seal しるし、イン	ノ	イ	′	′	臼	印		

A hand ⺕ is pressing on the head of a kneeling man ⼘.

印	しるし	mark
印	いん	seal
	… ◇ …	
印税	いんぜい	royalty

145 刷	print サツ、（サッ）	コ	コ	尸	尸	局	刷	刷	

A person 尸 with a knife 刂 prints on a stencil 巾.

印刷する	いんさつする	to print
	… ◇ …	
印刷物	いんさつぶつ	printed matter
刷新する	さっしんする	to reform

146 換	substitute, replace カン	一	扌	扌	扌′	扩	护	拘
		拘	捣	換	換			

A big 大 man ク with a big chest 四 can work 扌, substituting for many people.

変換する	へんかんする	to change
置換する	ちかんする	to replace
	… ◇ …	
交換する	こうかんする	to exchange

---

147 選　choose

えら・ぶ、セン

フ	コ	己	己フ	己コ	己己	己己	罕

| 罕 | 罢 | 巽 | 巽 | `巽 | 選 | 選 | |

Two men 己己 and two hands 共 represent many people. Thus 選 means to go ⻌ and choose one out of many candidates.

選ぶ	えらぶ	to choose
選択する	せんたくする	to choose
	… ◇ …	
選手	せんしゅ	player

---

148 検　investigate, inspect

ケン

一	十	才	木	朳	朳	衿	柃

| 柃 | 柃 | 棆 | 検 | | | | |

This kanji means to investigate the quality of a mound 僉 of wood 木.

検索する	けんさくする	to search
	… ◇ …	
検診	けんしん	medical examination
検定	けんてい	official approval
検事	けんじ	public prosecutor

---

149 了　finish

リョウ

フ	了						

This is a pictograph of the last part of a thread. Thus 了 means to end.

終了する	しゅうりょうする	to quit, to end
	… ◇ …	
修了する	しゅうりょうする	to complete (a course)

4 PRACTICE

Ⅰ. Write the readings of the following kanji in hiragana.

1. 漢 字　　　　　2. 編 集　　　　　3. 英 数　　　　　4. 新 規

5. 削 除　　　　　6. 印 刷　　　　　7. 変 換　　　　　8. 選 択^{たく}

9. 検 索^{さく}　　　　10. 終 了

11. この中から、好きなものを選んでください。

12. ここに、印をつけてください。

13. 英語は、多くの国で話されています。

14. ジャネットさんは、交換留学生です。

Ⅱ. Fill in the blanks with appropriate kanji.

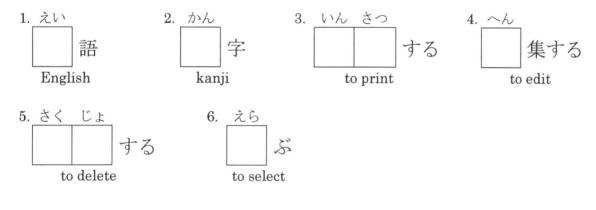

1. えい
　□ 語
English

2. かん
　□ 字
kanji

3. いん さつ
　□ □ する
to print

4. へん
　□ 集する
to edit

5. さく じょ
　□ □ する
to delete

6. えら
　□ ぶ
to select

129

5 SUPPLEMENT

ファイル(F)

新規作成(N)	Ctrl+N
開く(O)	Ctrl+O
閉じる(C)	
上書き保存(S)	Ctrl+S
名前を付けて保存(A)	
すべて保存(L)	
プロパティ(I)	
テンプレート(T)	
ページ設定(U)	
印刷プレビュー(V)	
印刷(P)	Ctrl+P
Microsoft Word　の終了(X)	

Some Words for Menus

新規作成	しんきさくせい	create
開く	ひらく	open
閉じる	とじる	close
上書き保存	うわがきほぞん	overwrite save
設定	せってい	set-up
印刷	いんさつ	print
終了	しゅうりょう	quit

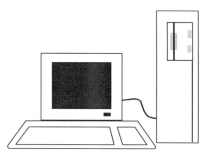

編集(E)

元に戻す(U)	Ctrl+Z
繰り返し(R)	Ctrl+Y
切り取り(T)	Ctrl+X
コピー(C)	Ctrl+C
貼り付け(P)	Ctrl+V
形式を選択して貼り付け(S)	
クリア(A)	Delete
すべてを選択(L)	Ctrl+A
検索(F)	Ctrl+F
置換(E)	Ctrl+H
ジャンプ(G)	Ctrl+G
オートテキスト(X)	
ブックマーク(B)	
日本語入力辞書への単語登録(I)	

編集	へんしゅう	edit
元に戻す	もとにもどす	restore
繰り返す	くりかえす	repeat
切り取り	きりとり	cut
貼り付け	はりつけ	paste
選択	せんたく	select
検索	けんさく	find
置換	ちかん	replace
罫線	けいせん	line
表示	ひょうじ	view
標準	ひょうじゅん	standard

挿入(I)

文書の区切り(B)	
ページ番号(U)	
注釈(A)	
日付と時刻(T)	
アドレス帳(C)	
フィールド(E)	
記号と文字(S)	
定型文書フィールド(M)	
脚注(N)	
図表番号(I)	
クロス　リファレンス(R)	
索引と目次(X)	
ファイル(L)	
レイアウト枠(E)	
図(P)	
オブジェクト(O)	
データベース(D)	
スタンプ(W)	

挿入	そうにゅう	insert
文書	ぶんしょ	sentence
日付	ひづけ	date
記号	きごう	mark, symbol
文字	もじ	letter
脚注	きゃくちゅう	footnote
図表番号	ずひょうばんごう	symbol number
索引	さくいん	index
目次	もくじ	content

書式(O)

文字(E)	
段落(P)	
タブ(T)	
段組み(C)	
縦書きと横書き(X)	
文字種変換(E)	
ドロップ　キャップ(D)	
箇条書きと段落番号(N)	
章番号(H)	
オートフォーマット(A)	
スタイル集(G)	
スタイル(S)	
レイアウト枠(M)	
図(R)	
描画オブジェクト(O)	

書式	しょしき	format
段落	だんらく	paragraph
段組み	だんぐみ	column
縦書き	たてがき	vertical
横書き	よこがき	horizontal
箇条書き	かじょうがき	itemize
描画	びょうが	drawing

Some Words for the Keyboard

変換	へんかん	conversion
無変換	むへんかん	non-conversion
半角	はんかく	half space
全角	ぜんかく	full space

Microwave Ovens　電子レンジ

でん　し
電子レンジ　　microwave oven

あたため　　warm up

なま　　かいとう
生もの解凍　　defrost

し　あが
仕上がり　　finish

きょう　　じゃく
強／弱　　strong/weak

しゅどう
手動　　manual

とりけし　　cancel

おん　ど　せってい
温度設定　　temperature setting

お
押す　スタート　push to start

旅行します

Reading Travel Brochures

JAPAN HAS many attractive tourist destinations.   Travel agencies offer various domestic tour packages that cover the cost of transportation, accommodations, and meals.   JR (Japan Railways) sells the Japan Rail Pass which permits unlimited travel on JR for a given period, but this pass can only be purchased abroad.   Alternatively, JR and some other railroad companies issue excursion tickets, coupon tickets, or special passes for a very reasonable price. Bus companies offer long-distance overnight bus service between major cities.   These options make traveling in Japan very easy, comfortable, and inexpensive.   Further information on travel within Japan can be obtained from tourist information centers in Tokyo and Kyoto and at international airports.

1　INTRODUCTORY QUIZ

Look at the illustration below and refer to the words in VOCABULARY. Then try the following quiz.

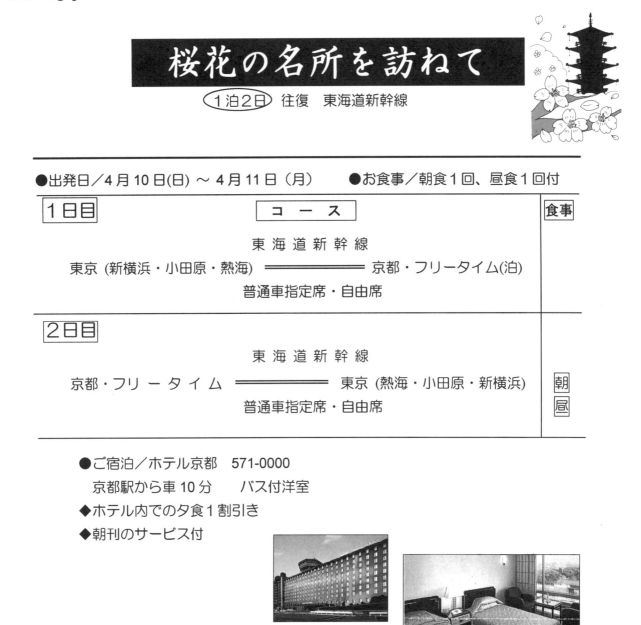

桜花の名所を訪ねて

①泊②日　往復　東海道新幹線

●出発日／4月10日(日) ～ 4月11日（月）　　　●お食事／朝食1回、昼食1回付

1日目	コース	食事
	東　海　道　新　幹　線 東京 (新横浜・小田原・熱海) ＝＝＝＝＝ 京都・フリータイム(泊) 普通車指定席・自由席	
2日目	東　海　道　新　幹　線 京都・フリータイム ＝＝＝＝＝ 東京 (熱海・小田原・新横浜) 普通車指定席・自由席	朝 昼

●ご宿泊／ホテル京都　571-0000
　京都駅から車10分　　バス付洋室
◆ホテル内での夕食1割引き
◆朝刊のサービス付

Read the above brochure from a travel agent and answer the following questions.

1. 京都へ、（ a. しんかんせん、　b. ひこうき ）で行きます。
2. 京都で、（ a. 一日、　b. 二日 ）泊まります。
3. 二日目は、（ a. 朝食、　b. 夕食 ）が付いています。

2 VOCABULARY

Study the readings and meanings of these words to help you understand the INTRODUCTORY QUIZ.

1.	1泊2日	いっ ぱく ふつ か	two-day trip, overnight trip
2.	往復	おう ふく	round trip
3.	東海道新幹線	とう かい どう しん かん せん	Tokaido super express/bullet train
4.	朝食	ちょう しょく	breakfast
5.	昼食	ちゅう しょく	lunch
6.	夕食	ゆう しょく	dinner, supper
7.	バス付	バス つき	with bath
8.	自由席	じ ゆう せき	nonreserved seat
9.	宿泊	しゅく はく	stay
10.	旅行代金	りょ こう だい きん	travel expense

3 NEW CHARACTERS

Ten characters are introduced in this lesson. Use the explanations to help you understand and remember the characters. Study the compound words to increase your vocabulary.

泊 宿 往 復 海 幹 朝 昼 夕 由

150 泊	stay; lodge と・まる、ハク、（パク）	丶	冫	氵	氵	泊	泊	泊	泊

A boat anchors in shallow, white 白 water 氵 to stay.	泊まる	とまる	to put up for the night
	一泊	いっぱく	overnight stay
	… ◇ …		
	泊まり客	とまりきゃく	houseguest

151 宿	lodging, inn やど、シュク、（ジュク）	` `` 宀 宀 宀 宀 宀 宿 宿 宿 宿

One hundred 百 people イ in a house 宀 indicates a lodge.	宿泊	しゅくはく	stay, lodging
	新宿	しんじゅく	Shinjuku (place name)
		… ◇ …	
	下宿する	げしゅくする	to board and lodge at a house
	合宿する	がっしゅくする	to stay together in a camp
	民宿	みんしゅく	pension
	宿屋	やどや	Japanese-style inn

152 往	go オウ	ノ ク イ 彳 彳 行 往 往

The man will go イ in a stately manner like a master 主.	往復	おうふく	round trip
		… ◇ …	
	車の往来	くるまのおうらい	vehicular traffic
	往復はがき	おうふくはがき	postage-paid reply card

153 復	return; be restored フク、（フッ）	ノ ク イ 彳 彳 彳 行 宿 宿 復 復 復

Go イ and turn 复 combine to mean return 復.		… ◇ …	
	回復する	かいふくする	to recover
	復元する	ふくげんする	to restore to the original
	復元力	ふくげんりょく	stability
	復活	ふっかつ	revival

154 海 — sea
うみ、カイ

Stroke order: 丶 氵 氵 氵 汇 汇 海 海 海 海

Every 毎 river or water 氵 empties into the sea.

海	うみ	sea
海水	かいすい	sea water
海外	かいがい	overseas
日本海	にほんかい	Sea of Japan

… ◇ …

東海道新幹線	とうかいどう しんかんせん	Tokaido super express
大海	たいかい	ocean

155 幹 — main part; trunk
みき、カン

Stroke order: 一 十 十 古 古 古 直 卓 卓 卓 幹 幹 幹

Tree trunks 幹 are used to dry the laundry 干 in the morning when the sun is low in the grass 十.

新幹線	しんかんせん	super express

… ◇ …

木の幹	きのみき	trunk
幹部	かんぶ	executive
幹事	かんじ	manager

156 朝 — morning
あさ、チョウ

Stroke order: 一 十 十 古 古 古 直 卓 卓 朝 朝 朝

In the morning, the sun 日 is between the trees 十 and the moon 月 can still be seen.

朝	あさ	morning
朝食	ちょうしょく	breakfast
毎朝	まいあさ	every morning

… ◇ …

朝日	あさひ	morning sun
朝日新聞	あさひしんぶん	Asahi Daily News

157 昼	daytime; noon ひる、チュウ	コ	コ	尸	尺	尺	尽	昼	昼
		昼							

尺 shows a man who is working bending over his shovel. 旦 shows that the sun is high. Thus 昼 means daytime when people work.

昼	ひる	daytime
昼食	ちゅうしょく	lunch
昼休み	ひるやすみ	lunchtime
昼ごはん	ひるごはん	lunch

… ◇ …

158 夕	evening ユウ	ノ	ク	夕					

This is a pictograph of the moon just above a mountain in the evening.

夕食	ゆうしょく	supper
夕方	ゆうがた	evening
夕日	ゆうひ	setting sun

… ◇ …

159 由	reason, cause ユウ	丨	冂	巾	由	由			

由 is the pictograph of a wine jar with the mouth protruding from the center, out of which wine is poured. Thus 由 means a cause of the outcome.

自由	じゆう	free
自由席	じゆうせき	nonreserved seat
不自由	ふじゆう	discomfort; want

… ◇ …

理由	りゆう	reason

4 PRACTICE

I. Write the readings of the following kanji in hiragana.

1. 一 泊 二 日　　2. 宿 泊　　　　3. 往 復　　　　4. 海 外

5. 新 幹 線　　　6. 朝 食　　　　7. 昼 食　　　　8. 夕 食

9. 指定席は、自由席より高いです。

10. 海に近い旅館に、泊まりたいです。

11. 次の日の朝早く、出発しました。

12. 昼ごろか、夕方に、到着するでしょう。

13. 私は、毎朝、6時におきます。

II. Fill in the blanks with appropriate kanji.

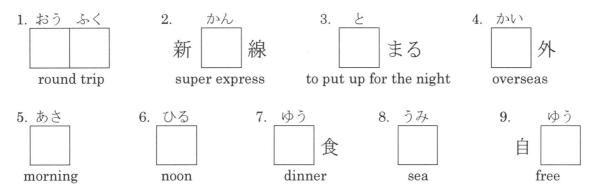

1. おう　ふく
　□□
round trip

2. かん
新□線
super express

3. と
□まる
to put up for the night

4. かい
□外
overseas

5. あさ
□
morning

6. ひる
□
noon

7. ゆう
□食
dinner

8. うみ
□
sea

9. ゆう
自□
free

Japan Sightseeing Map　日本観光地図

日本観光地図

札幌

青森

十和田湖

仙台

金沢　日光

長野

広島　京都　横浜　東京

長崎　大分　奈良　鎌倉

熊本

温泉に行きます

Sightseeing Buses and Hot-Spring Baths

TRAVELERS IN Japan have a wide range of overnight lodgings from which to choose. You can choose from Western-style hotels, Japanese-style inns called *ryokan,* small private pensions called *minshuku,* youth hostels, or even campgrounds. Japanese-style inns usually have extra large, communal baths, one for men and one for women. In hot-spring resorts, there are often large, open-air hot-spring baths, designed to enable guests to enjoy beautiful scenery as they bathe.

1 INTRODUCTORY QUIZ

Look at the illustration below, and refer to the words in VOCABULARY. Then try the following quiz.

Ⅰ. As Mike and Mary have free time on the first day, they want to take a sightseeing bus. Which route do you think is the best for them, A, B, or C?

京都定期観光バス

A 京の半日	B 京の3寺めぐり	C 京の一日
金 閣 寺 ↓ 清 水 寺 ↓ 平 安 神 宮 ↓ 知 恩 院	金 閣 寺 ↓ 銀 閣 寺 ↓ 清 水 寺	金 閣 寺 ↓ 銀 閣 寺 ↓ 清 水 寺 ↓ 平 安 神 宮 ↓ 三十三間堂
大人　5,200 円 小児　2,850 円	大人　4,350 円 小児　2,500 円	大人　7,300 円 小児　3,950 円
約 5時間	約 3時間半	約 6時間半
9:30　10:00　10:30 11:00　11:30　12:00	9:20　12:20　13:20	9:00　9:30

Ⅱ. At the Japanese-style inn, there is a big bath for women only and one for men only. Which bath should Mary take? And how about Mike? Write the letters (a〜d) in the spaces provided.

1. メアリー（　　）（　　）　2. マイク（　　）（　　）

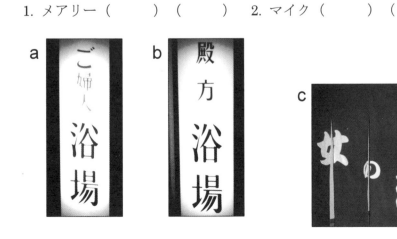

a　ご婦人浴場
b　殿方浴場
c　女の湯

d　男の湯

2 | VOCABULARY

Study the readings and meanings of these words to help you understand the INTRODUC-
TORY QUIZ.

1. 定期観光バス　　　てい き かん こう バス　　　regular sightseeing bus
2. 金閣寺　　　　　　きん かく じ　　　　　　　Golden Pavilion temple
3. 清水寺　　　　　　きよ みず でら　　　　　　Kiyomizudera temple
4. 平安神宮　　　　　へい あん じん ぐう　　　　Heianjingu shrine
5. 知恩院　　　　　　ち おん いん　　　　　　　Chionin temple
6. 銀閣寺　　　　　　ぎん かく じ　　　　　　　Silver Pavilion temple
7. 三十三間堂　　　　さん じゅう さん げん どう　Sanjusangendo temple
8. 大人　　　　　　　おとな　　　　　　　　　　adult
9. 小児　　　　　　　しょう に　　　　　　　　　child
10. 大浴場　　　　　　だい よく じょう　　　　　big bath
11. 婦人　　　　　　　ふ じん　　　　　　　　　　ladies
12. 殿方　　　　　　　との がた　　　　　　　　　gentlemen
13. 温泉　　　　　　　おん せん　　　　　　　　　hot spring

3 | NEW CHARACTERS

Eight characters are introduced in this lesson.　Use the explanations to help you understand
and remember the characters.　Study the compound words to increase your vocabulary.

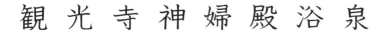

観 光 寺 神 婦 殿 浴 泉

| 160 観 | look, observe
カン | ノ | ヒ | ヒ | ゲ | 午 | 矢 | 卒 | 弁 |
| | | 奔 | 奎 | 雀 | 観目 | 観見 | 観見 | | |

Look 見 at the fat bird 隹 with a hat ケ.

観光	かんこう	sightseeing
観光客	かんこうきゃく	tourist
	… ◇ …	
観×察する	かんさつする	to observe
主×観	しゅかん	subjective view
客観	きゃっかん	objective view
外観	がいかん	outside appearance

| 161 光 | light; shine
ひかり、コウ | ノ | ソ | ツ | 业 | 半 | 光 | | |
| | | | | | | | | | |

This is a pictograph of light.

光	ひかり	light
日光	にっこう	sunlight, Nikko (place name)
光学	こうがく	optics
	… ◇ …	
光線	こうせん	beam

| 162 寺 | temple
てら、（でら）、ジ | 一 | 十 | 土 | 圭 | 寺 | 寺 | | |
| | | | | | | | | | |

Soil 土 and hand 寸 suggest work. A place where priests work is a temple.

寺	てら	temple
	… ◇ …	
銀×閣寺	ぎんかくじ	Silver Pavilion temple
金×閣寺	きんかくじ	Golden Pavilion temple
清水寺	きよみずでら	Kiyomizudera temple

| 163 神 | god; shrine かみ、ジン | ヽ | ラ | ネ | ネ | ネ | 初 | 初 | 神 |
| | | 神 | | | | | | | |

神 combines altar ネ and heavenly speech 申.	神	かみ	god
	神様	かみさま	god
	神社	じんじゃ	shrine
	… ◇ …		
	神宮	じんぐう	shrine

| 164 婦 | woman; wife フ | く | 夕 | 女 | 女' | 女ヲ | 女ヨ | 妒 | 婦 |
| | | 婦 | 婦 | 婦 | | | | | |

A woman 女 with a broom 帚 is an adult woman.	主婦	しゅふ	housewife
	婦人	ふじん	lady
	婦人科	ふじんか	gynecology
	… ◇ …		
	夫婦	ふうふ	married couple

| 165 殿 | gentleman; Mr., Mrs., Miss; hall, palace との、どの、テン、デン | フ | コ | 尸 | 尸 | 尺 | 屏 | 屉 | 屏 |
| | | 屐 | 屍 | 殿 | 殿 | 殿 | | | |

Individual persons 尸 getting together 共 to fight 殳 for a lord. Thus 殿 also means the lord's palace. Now 殿 also means a gentleman.	殿方	とのがた	gentleman
	田中殿	たなかどの	Mr./Ms. Tanaka
	… ◇ …		
	殿下	でんか	His Highness
	御殿	ごてん	palace

166 浴	bathe ヨク	丶	ニ	シ	ニ	ニ	ニ	氵	氵
		浴	浴						

Valley 谷 and water 氵 combined, 浴 suggests a hollow space in which to accumulate water for a bath. Thus 浴 means to bathe.	大浴場	だいよくじょう	big bath
	海水浴場	かいすいよくじょう	beach
		… ◇ …	
	日光浴	にっこうよく	sunbathing

167 泉	spring いずみ、セン	ノ	イ	白	白	白	皀	泉	泉
		泉							

White 白 and water 水 combined, 泉 means a spring whose water is clear and white.	泉	いずみ	spring
	温泉	おんせん	hot spring
		… ◇ …	
	源泉	げんせん	fountainhead

4 PRACTICE

I . Write the readings of the following kanji in hiragana.

1. 観 光   2. 田 中 殿   3. 日 光   4. 婦 人

5. 殿 方   6. 大 浴 場   7. 温 泉   8. 神 様

9. 京都は、神社やお寺が多いです。

10. 毎年、八月に、海水浴に行きます。

11. 海や山は、光が強いです。

12. 手紙^{がみ}の時、スミス様とスミス殿と、どちらがいいですか。

13. 外ではたらいている主婦は、多いそうです。

Ⅱ. Fill in the blanks with appropriate kanji.

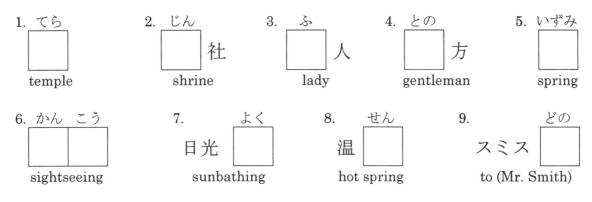

1. てら
　□
　temple

2. じん
　□社
　shrine

3. ふ
　□人
　lady

4. との
　□方
　gentleman

5. いずみ
　□
　spring

6. かん　こう
　□□
　sightseeing

7. よく
　日光□
　sunbathing

8. せん
　温□
　hot spring

9. どの
　スミス□
　to (Mr. Smith)

REVIEW EXERCISE   Lessons 10−15

I. Find the correct words from the box below and write their corresponding letters in the parentheses.

1. 先週（　　　　）で、京都へ行きました。

2. 観光バスにのって、（　　　　）や（　　　　）を見ました。

3. ビデオを見るとき、（　　　　）ボタンを押します。

4. 食器を洗うとき、（　　　　）を使います。

5. 名古屋まで（　　　　）のきっぷを買いました。

6. あついですから、エアコンの（　　　　）ボタンを押してください。

7. （　　　　）や（　　　　）は、よく洗ってから食べましょう。

```
  a. 再生      b. 寺        c. 往復      d. 果物      e. 冷房

  f. 新幹線    g. 台所洗剤   h. 野菜      i. 神社
```

II. The words listed below relate to one of five categories. Group them appropriately and write their letters in the spaces provided.

1. ビデオ　　　　　　（　　　）（　　　）（　　　）

2. パソコン　　　　　（　　　）（　　　）（　　　）

3. 旅行　　　　　　　（　　　）（　　　）（　　　）

4. 洗濯　　　　　　　（　　　）（　　　）（　　　）

5. ルームエアコン　　（　　　）（　　　）（　　　）

```
  a. 毛        b. 印刷      c. 冷房      d. 新幹線    e. 早送り

  f. 観光バス  g. 洗剤      h. 終了      i. 録画      j. 一泊二日

  k. 削除      l. 運転      m. 再生      n. 綿        o. 暖房
```

車を運転します

Driving on the Expressways

DO YOU like driving? It is a lot of fun to go by car from northernmost Hokkaido to the southern tip of Kyushu. Big cities in Japan are connected by expressways and local roads. The first tollway between Nagoya (Komaki) and Kobe (Nishinomiya) was constructed in 1965, followed by the Tomei Expressway between Tokyo and Nagoya. These two trunk highways linking the busiest cities made faster cargo distribution possible and assured easier and more comfortable driving. The beginning of the highway-driving era coincided with the birth of the Shinkansen, a new Tokaido Line between Tokyo and Osaka. The new highways and train service enabled comfortable, quick transportation for business people and other travelers. Although highway signs are mostly written in both Japanese and romaji, emergency warnings, or flashing highway information on electric bulletin boards, such as "Accident Ahead, Slow Down," are usually given in Japanese only. If you can understand those words on the board, you can react quickly to avert possible danger. In this lesson, you will learn the words to be sure your driving on the expressways is safe.

1 INTRODUCTORY QUIZ

Look at the illustrations below and refer to the words in VOCABULARY. Then try the following quiz.

You will see many signs on highways or local roads. Match the signs with the meanings and write the correct letters (a~k) in the parentheses.

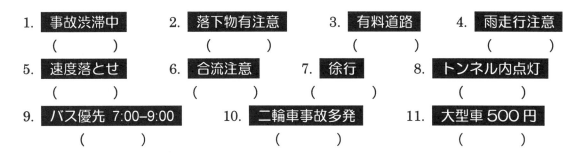

1. 事故渋滞中　　2. 落下物有注意　　3. 有料道路　　4. 雨走行注意
　　(　　　)　　　　　(　　　)　　　　(　　　)　　　　(　　　)

5. 速度落とせ　　6. 合流注意　　7. 徐行　　8. トンネル内点灯
　　(　　　)　　　　(　　　)　　　(　　　)　　　　(　　　)

9. バス優先 7:00–9:00　　10. 二輪車事故多発　　11. 大型車 500 円
　　(　　　)　　　　　　　　　(　　　)　　　　　　　(　　　)

a. Slow down.

b. Turn on lights in tunnel.

c. Toll road.

d. Two-wheeled vehicle frequent accidents.

e. Watch for fallen objects.

f. Bus priority lane: 7:00–9:00.

g. Reduce speed.

h. Large-sized vehicles: ¥500.

i. Caution: merging traffic.

j. Accident; congestion.

k. Rain, drive carefully.

2 VOCABULARY

Study the readings and meanings of these words to help you understand the INTRODUCTORY QUIZ.

1.	事故	じ こ	accident
2.	渋滞中	じゅう たい ちゅう	congestion
3.	落下物有	らっ か ぶつ あり	fallen object
4.	徐行	じょ こう	Slow down.
5.	走行	そう こう	driving, traveling
6.	速度落とせ	そく ど お とせ	Reduce speed.
7.	合流	ごう りゅう	merging
8.	有料道路	ゆう りょう どう ろ	toll road
9.	点灯	てん とう	Turn on lights.
10.	優先	ゆう せん	priority
11.	二輪車	に りん しゃ	two-wheeled vehicle
12.	事故多発	じ こ た はつ	frequent accidents

| 13. | 大型車 | おお がた しゃ | large-sized vehicle |
| 14. | 高速道路 | こう そく どう ろ | expressway |

3 NEW CHARACTERS

Eleven characters are introduced in this lesson. Use the explanations to help you understand and remember the characters. Study the compound words to increase your vocabulary.

路 優 輪 徐 点 型 落 渋 滞 流 走

168 路 ロ	road	⟍	⼝	⼝	𧾷	𧾷	𧾷	𧾷	𧾷
		跂	趵	趵	路	路			

Everyone 各 walks 足 on the road.	道路	どうろ	road
		… ◇ …	
	通路	つうろ	passage
	路面電車	ろめんでんしゃ	streetcar
	線路	せんろ	railway

169 優 やさ・しい、ユウ	kindhearted, gentle; excel	⼃	⼈	亻	亻	亻	佰	佰	佰
		佰	価	傊	慐	優	優	優	

憂 means grief, because the head and the heart 心 are grieving and the legs are trailing behind. To grieve 憂 for someone else イ is kindheartedness 優.	優しい	やさしい	kindhearted
	優先	ゆうせん	priority
		… ◇ …	
	優良な	ゆうりょうな	superior
	女優	じょゆう	actress

151

---

170 輪 wheel, circle, ring
わ、リン

一 厂 厅 亓 自 車 車 軸 軸 軸 軸 軩 輪 輪

侖 is a pictograph of the spokes of a wheel emphasizing a circle and regularity. Wheel 車 is added to reinforce the meaning.

輪	わ	ring
二輪車	にりんしゃ	two-wheeled vehicle
… ◇ …		
五輪	ごりん	Olympic Games
指輪	ゆびわ	ring

---

171 徐 slowly
ジョ

ノ ク 彳 彳 彳 徐 徐 徐 徐 徐

余 means leftover or excessive. 徐 is to go 彳 slowly without excessive speed.

徐行する	じょこうする	to go/to drive slowly
… ◇ …		
徐々に	じょじょに	gradually

---

172 点 point
テン

一 ト 片 占 占 点 点 点 点

Fortunetellers 占 burn 灬 bones ト, leaving black points or spots, by which they make a prediction.

点灯する	てんとうする	to light (a lamp)
百点	ひゃくてん	mark of 100
… ◇ …		
点火する	てんかする	to ignite
点字	てんじ	Braille
利点	りてん	advantage

173 型	form, model かた、（がた）、ケイ	一	二	乒	开	开l	开l	型l	型
		型							

Clay 土 is molded into a form 型 using a stick 一, two hands 开, and a knife 刂 .

大型	おおがた	large
中型	ちゅうがた	medium
小型	こがた	small
	… ◇ …	
文型	ぶんけい	sentence pattern

174 落	fall おち・る、お・とす、ラク、（ラッ）	一	十	サ	艹	茫	茫	艻	茺
		茨	茨	落	落				

Each 各 raindrop 氵 on the leaves 艹 falls 落 onto the ground.

落ちる	おちる	to fall
落下物	らっかぶつ	falling object, fallen object
速度落とせ	そくどおとせ	Reduce speed.
	… ◇ …	

175 渋	astringent; pucker; reluctant しぶ、ジュウ	丶	冫	氵	氵	氵	氵	氵	渋
		渋	渋	渋					

Water 氵 stops 止 behind a dam.

渋滞	じゅうたい	traffic jam
	… ◇ …	
渋谷	しぶや	Shibuya (place name)

| 176 滞 | stay タイ | 丶 | ⺀ | シ | 氵 | 汁 | 沪 | 沪 | 泄 |
| | | 泄 | 滞 | 滞 | 滞 | 滞 | | | |

帯 is a pictograph for a belt. Water 氵 stays 滞 in a long narrow lake.

滞在する	たいざいする	to stay

… ◇ …

| 177 流 | current; style なが・れる、なが・す、リュウ | 丶 | ⺀ | シ | シ | 氵 | 汢 | 泸 | 浐 |
| | | 流 | 流 | | | | | | |

㐬 is a newborn baby, with its head upside down, with the meaning of "flowing" added. Water 氵 is added to reinforce the meaning of flowing.

流れる	ながれる	to flow
流す	ながす	to let (water) flow
		to flush, to drain
合流	ごうりゅう	merging traffic
一流	いちりゅう	first class

… ◇ …

流行	りゅうこう	fashion
上流	じょうりゅう	upstream, upper class

| 178 走 | run はし・る、ソウ | 一 | 十 | 土 | キ | キ | 走 | 走 | |
| | | | | | | | | | |

This is a pictograph of a man with his arms stretched out.

走る	はしる	to run
走行注意	そうこうちゅうい	Drive carefully.

… ◇ …

4 PRACTICE

Ⅰ. Write the readings of the following kanji in hiragana.

1. 走 行 注 意   2. 優 先   3. 二 輪 車   4. 徐 行

5. 渋 滞   6. 合 流   7. 点 灯

8. バスやトラックは、大型車です。

9. 雨なので、速度を落としてください。

10. 山中さんは、優しい人です。

11. 走らないで、ゆっくり歩きましょう。

12. 道路が、渋滞しています。

13. 水を流してください。

14. 漢字のテストで、100点をとりました。

Ⅱ. Fill in the blanks with appropriate kanji.

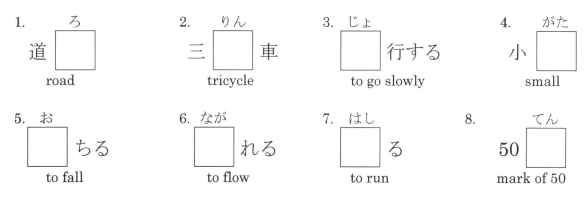

1. ろ
道 □
road

2. りん
三 □ 車
tricycle

3. じょ
□ 行する
to go slowly

4. がた
小 □
small

5. お
□ ちる
to fall

6. なが
□ れる
to flow

7. はし
□ る
to run

8. てん
50 □
mark of 50

5 SUPPLEMENT

Highway Signs

Rain
Caution Slippery

Strong Winds
Drive Carefully

Snow
Caution Slippery

Fatal Accident Zone
Reduce Speed

Drive Carefully
Road Under Construction

Congestion, 1 km Ahead

Rain, Drive Carefully

1 km Congested Traffic

Tunnel Information
Reduce Speed
Under Construction

Turn on Lights

天気予報

How to Read Weather Forecasts

Courtesy of *Yomiuri Shimbun.*

WEATHER FORECASTS are printed in the newspaper every morning and every evening. If you know some of the relevant kanji, you can make plans according to today's or tomorrow's weather. Seasons in Japan are usually quite consistent. Spring, from March to May, is pleasantly warm, while summers are hot and humid from July to August. The rainy season extends from the middle of June to the middle of July, and heavy showers fall occasionally throughout the rest of the summer. Typhoons are common in Japan between July and September. It is cool and fresh during the autumn months, from September to November, although September weather can be unpredictable. December is likely to be cold and clear, while the end of January to the end of February can be especially cold in many areas of Japan. In December, there are heavy snowfalls along the Japan Sea Coast and in Hokkaido.

1 INTRODUCTORY QUIZ

Look at the illustrations below and refer to the words in VOCABULARY. Then try the following quiz.

夏 の 天 気

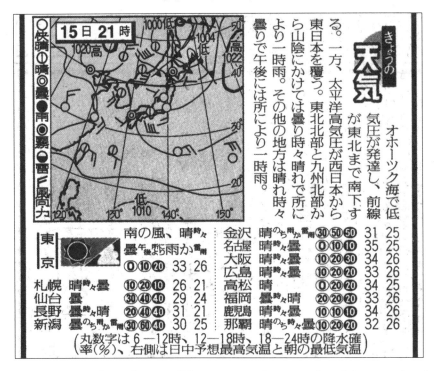

I. Look at the summer weather above. The two numbers at the right are the day's high and low temperatures. Discuss and answer the following questions.

1. 一番あつい所は、どこでしょう。

2. 一番すずしい所は、どこでしょう。

3. きょうの東京の天気は、どうですか。

冬の天気の記号
Weather symbols in winter

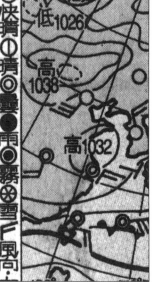

II. Match the following symbols and meanings.
Write the correct letters (a～f) in the spaces provided.

1. ○ : (　　　)   a. ゆ き

2. ⦶ : (　　　)   b. ふうこう／りょく

3. ◎ : (　　　)   c. かいせい

4. ● : (　　　)   d. くもり

5. ⊗ : (　　　)   e. は れ

6. F : (　　　)   f. あ め

Weather charts courtesy of *Yomiuri Shimbun*.

2 VOCABULARY

Study the readings and meanings of these words to help you understand the INTRODUCTORY QUIZ.

1.	天気予報	てん き よ ほう	weather forecast
2.	夏	なつ	summer
3.	冬	ふゆ	winter
4.	快晴	かい せい	very clear weather
5.	晴	はれ	clear weather
6.	曇	くもり	cloudy weather
7.	雨	あめ	rain
8.	霧×	きり	fog
9.	雷×	かみなり	thunder
10.	雪	ゆき	snow
11.	風向	ふう こう	wind direction
12.	風力	ふう りょく	wind strength
13.	数字	すう じ	numeral
14.	右側	みぎ がわ	right side
15.	日中	にっ ちゅう	daytime
16.	最高気温	さい こう き おん	highest temperature (today's high)
17.	最低気温	さい てい き おん	lowest temperature (today's low)
18.	高気圧	こう き あつ	high air pressure
19.	低気圧	てい き あつ	low air pressure
20.	台風	たい ふう	typhoon
21.	時々	とき どき	sometimes
22.	所により	ところ により	partially, depends on the area
23.	一時	いち じ	briefly, temporarily

3 NEW CHARACTERS

Fifteen characters are introduced in this lesson. Use the explanations to help you understand and remember the characters. Study the compound words to increase your vocabulary.

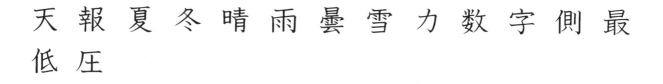

天 報 夏 冬 晴 雨 曇 雪 力 数 字 側 最
低 圧

179 天	heaven テン	一	二	天	天				

A big 大 person is holding the sky 一 above him/her.

天気	てんき	weather
	… ◇ …	
雨天	うてん	rainy weather
天国	てんごく	paradise
天使	てんし	angel

---

180 報	news; report ホウ、（ポウ）	一	十	土	圭	吉	赱	查	幸
		幸ﾞ	郣	報	報				

Land 土 or yen ¥ was the reward 報 traditionally given to the person 阝 bearing information or news. The person received the reward with his hand 又. Thus 報 means to report.

天気予報	てんきよほう	weather forecast
電報	でんぽう	telegraph
	… ◇ …	
速報	そくほう	news flash
報道する	ほうどうする	to report news

---

181 夏	summer なつ、カ	一	丆	丆	百	百	百	頁
		夏	夏					

Head 首 and legs 夊 suggest the dance of a summer festival.

夏	なつ	summer
	… ◇ …	
夏期	かき	summer period
夏物	なつもの	summer clothing

182 冬

winter

ふゆ、トウ

ノ	ク	夂	冬	冬			

冬 depicts foods being hung up outdoors in the cold wind in winter for storage.

冬	ふゆ	winter

… ◇ …

真冬	まふゆ	midwinter
冬向き	ふゆむき	for winter
冬物	ふゆもの	winter clothing
冬期	とうき	winter period
暖冬	だんとう	warm winter

183 晴

clear up

は・れる、セイ

亅	冂	日	日	日	日	日	日
晴	晴	晴	晴				

晴 is a combination of the sun 日 and transparent 青. This is how the sky looks on a fine day.

晴れ	はれ	fine
晴天	せいてん	fine
快晴	かいせい	clear

… ◇ …

184 雨

rain

あめ、ウ

一	冂	冂	币	雨	雨	雨	雨

雨 is the pictograph of rain as raindrops fall from the clouds.

雨	あめ	rain
大雨	おおあめ	heavy rain

… ◇ …

雨期	うき	rainy season
雨天中止	うてんちゅうし	canceled in case of rain

| 185 曇 cloudy くも・る | １ | 冂 | 冃 | 日 | 旦 | 昮 | 昴 | 昴 |
| | 昴 | 昴 | 晏 | 晏 | 曇 | 曇 | 曇 | 曇 |

曇 is the combination of rain 雨 and something foggy 云. 雲 clouds hide 日 the sun, so it is cloudy.

| 曇り | くもり | cloudy |
| | … ◇ … | |

| 186 雪 snow ゆき、セツ | 一 | 一 | 戸 | 乕 | 乕 | 乕 | 雨 | 雨 |
| | 雫 | 雪 | 雪 | | | | | |

The falling rain 雨 combined with a picture of a broom ヨ means snow, because a broom was used to sweep the snow away.

雪	ゆき	snow
大雪	おおゆき	heavy snowfall
	… ◇ …	
新雪	しんせつ	new-fallen snow

| 187 力 power ちから、リキ、リョク | フ | 力 | | | | | | |
| | | | | | | | | |

力 depicts a strong man's arm, which indicates power.

風力	ふうりょく	wind power
電力	でんりょく	electric power
体力	たいりょく	physical strength
水力	すいりょく	water power
全力	ぜんりょく	utmost effort
	… ◇ …	
力	ちから	power
人力車	じんりきしゃ	rickshaw

188 数	number; count かず、スウ、（ズウ）	丶	丷	丷	半	半	米	娄	娄
		娄	娄	数	数	数			

Eighty-eight 八＋八＝米 women 女 are engaged in a number 数 of actions 攵.

数	かず	number
多数の	たすうの	many
人数	にんずう	number of people
手数料	てすうりょう	commission
数学	すうがく	mathematics
	… ◇ …	
無数の	むすうの	numerous
分数	ぶんすう	fraction

189 字	character, letter ジ	丶	宀	宀	字	字	字		

A child 子 is practicing writing letters in the house 宀.

数字	すうじ	numeral
文字	もじ	letter
字引	じびき	dictionary
	… ◇ …	
漢字	かんじ	kanji
字体	じたい	form of a character
当て字	あてじ	kanji used phonetically
十字	じゅうじ	cross

190 側	side かわ、（がわ）	ノ	イ	仏	们	佣	佃	佃	俱
		俱	俱	側					

A cooking vessel 貝 and a knife 刂 attached to a man イ means nearby or side.

右側	みぎがわ	right side
外側	そとがわ	outside
両側	りょうがわ	both sides
向こう側	むこうがわ	other side
	… ◇ …	
右側通行	みぎがわつうこう	Keep to the right.

191 最	the most, highest サイ	丶	冂	冃	日	旦	早	寻	昌
		昌	骨	最	最				

取 combines ear 耳 and hand 又. Ancient Chinese warriors used to cut the ears off their conquered enemies. Now 取 means to take. To take the sun 日 is the most 最 difficult thing to do.

最高	さいこう	highest
最後	さいご	last
最大	さいだい	biggest
最終	さいしゅう	last
最新	さいしん	newest
	… ◇ …	

192 低	low ひく・い、テイ	ノ	イ	イ	化	化	低	低	

氏 means family and thus means a person by emphasizing the lower part. In addition, combined with イ, 低 means a short person. Thus 低 means low.

低い	ひくい	low
最低	さいてい	lowest
	… ◇ …	
低所得	ていしょとく	low income
低成長	ていせいちょう	low growth
低地	ていち	lowland

193 圧	press アツ、（アッ）	一	厂	厂	斤	圧			

Soil 土 under a rocky cliff 厂 is pressed firmly.

高気圧	こうきあつ	high atmospheric pressure
低気圧	ていきあつ	low atmospheric pressure
圧力	あつりょく	pressure
	… ◇ …	
圧する	あっする	to press

4　PRACTICE

Ⅰ. Write the readings of the following kanji in hiragana.

1. 天 気 予 報 　　2. 夏 　　　　3. 冬 　　　　4. 晴 れ 　　5. 雨

6. 曇 り 　　　　　　7. 雪 　　　8. 風 力 　　9. 数 字 　　10. 右 側

11. 最 低 　　　　12. 高 気 圧 　　　　13. 低 い

14. 手数料は、いくらですか。

15. 日本で、人口が最大の都市は、東京です。

16. ここは、冬に雪が多いです。

Ⅱ. Fill in the blanks with appropriate kanji.

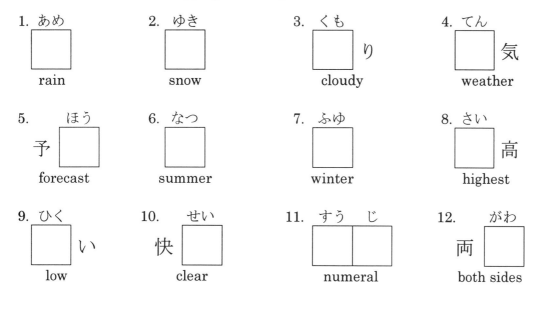

1. あめ
rain

2. ゆき
snow

3. くも
り
cloudy

4. てん
気
weather

5. ほう
予
forecast

6. なつ
summer

7. ふゆ
winter

8. さい
高
highest

9. ひく
い
low

10. せい
快
clear

11. すう じ
numeral

12. がわ
両
both sides

5　SUPPLEMENT

Ⅰ. There are some interesting words related to weather.

春一番　　　はる いち ばん　　　　　the first southern storm (strong wind) of the year,
　　　　　　　　　　　　　　　　　　usually arriving after mid-February

真夏日	ま なつ び	mid-summer day, temperature above 30℃
熱帯夜	ねっ たい や	tropical night, temperature above 25℃
不快指数	ふ かい し すう	discomfort index
小春日和	こ はる びより	warm autumn weather, Indian summer
桜前線	さくら ぜん せん	"The cherry blossom front" is the line showing where cherry trees are starting to bloom, based on the forecast by the Meteorological Agency.

お花見早くできそう

関東のサクラ
下旬ごろ開花

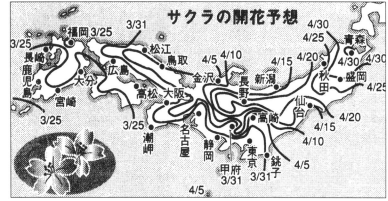

Courtesy of *Asahi Shimbun.*

Ⅱ. How many kanji do you know that have rain 雨 in them?

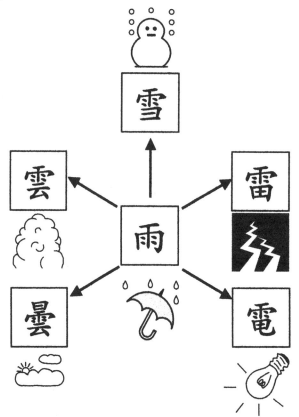

年賀状を書きましょう

Sending Cards

MUCH AS elsewhere in the world, Japanese people send greeting cards to mark special occasions such as births, to say thank you, or to notify friends of a change of address. But the most important, the most obligatory, of these is the *nengajo,* or New Year's card. A New Year's card is similar to a Christmas card, but the big difference is the date of its arrival. All New Year's cards are supposed to be delivered on the first day of January. Thus, at year end, Japanese people are busy writing tens or hundreds of New Year's cards to their colleagues, relatives, and business associates, so that they can be delivered on time. In this lesson, you will learn how to write a New Year's card and how to reply to an invitation card.

1 INTRODUCTORY QUIZ

Look at the illustrations below and refer to the words in VOCABULARY. Then try the following quiz.

Ⅰ. With the New Year approaching, Mike and Mary are busy writing New Year's cards （年賀状） to their friends. Try to write a card to your teacher, following the example.

Example

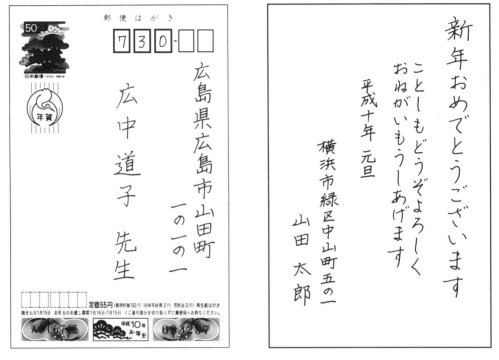

Note: When you write to people called *sensei*, write 先生 *(sensei)* in place of 様 *(sama)*.

Ⅱ. Mike received an invitation to a wedding （結婚式の招待状） with a return postcard from Mr. Yamada. He sends the reply card, saying that he is very happy to attend. You can send your own reply card following the example.

Example   返信用　おもて   返信用　うら

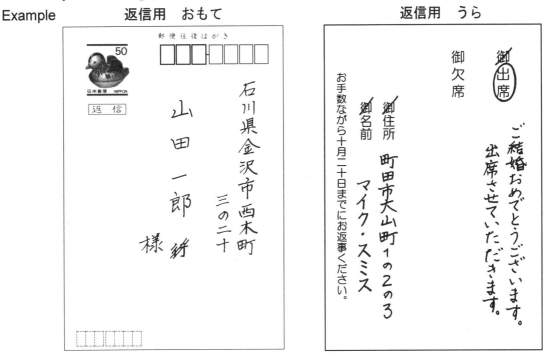

Note: When sending a reply card, you should do these things:

1. Cross out 行 *(iki)* of the sender and write 様 *(sama)*. In case the receiver is a company or an organization, write 御中 *(onchu)* in place of 様 *(sama)*.
2. Cross out all occurrences of the honorific character 御.
3. In the case of an invitation card, add a little message instead of just marking whether you will attend or not.

返信用　おもて   返信用　うら

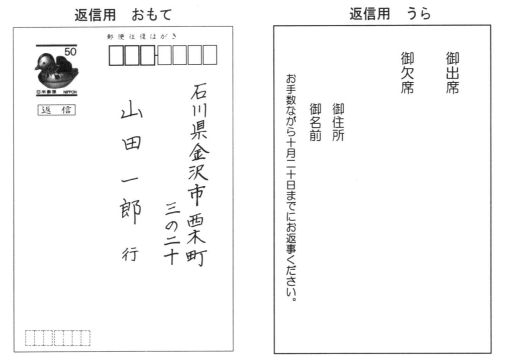

169

Note: If no one is at home when the postal service attempts to deliver a parcel or registered mail, they will leave a card called a "Notification of Attempted Delivery" in your mailbox. To claim your parcel, visit the post office named on the card and present some identification, such as your alien registration card, and the notification card.   The postal clerk will ask you to sign for the package or mail and then it will be given to you.

不在配達通知   Notification of Attempted Delivery

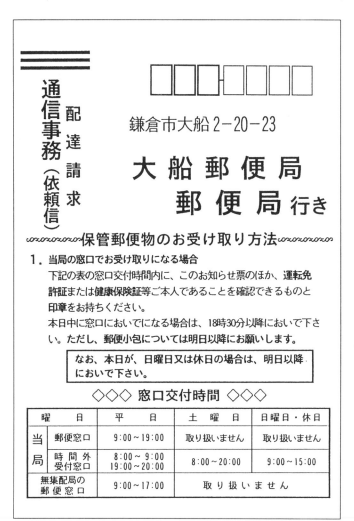

2 VOCABULARY

Study the readings and meanings of these words to help you understand the INTRODUCTORY QUIZ.

1.	年賀状	ねん が じょう	New Year's card
2.	元旦	がん たん	New Year's day (January 1st)

3.	広島県	ひろ しま けん	Hiroshima Prefecture
4.	結婚式	けっ こん しき	wedding ceremony
5.	招待状³	しょう たい じょう	invitation card
6.	返信	へん しん	reply
7.	御欠席	ご けっ せき	your (honorable) absence
8.	御出席	ご しゅっ せき	your (honorable) presence
9.	御名前	お な まえ	your (honorable) name
10.	～行き	～ い き	To ～
11.	～御中	～ おん ちゅう	Messrs. ～
12.	配達	はい たつ	delivery
13.	請求⁴	せい きゅう	claim
14.	窓口	まど ぐち	window
15.	不在配達通知	ふ ざい はい たつ つう ち	notification of attempted delivery

3 NEW CHARACTERS

Sixteen characters are introduced in this lesson. Use the explanations to help you understand and remember the characters. Study the compound words to increase your vocabulary.

賀 状 広 島 県 結 婚 招 返 信 御 欠 配
達 求 窓

194 賀	congratulations ガ	フ	カ	カl	カ口	カ口	加	智	賀
		智	智	賀	賀				

賀 combines add 加 and money 貝, thus meaning congratulations.	年賀状	ねんがじょう	New Year's card
		⋯ ◇ ⋯	
	賀状	がじょう	New Year's card
	賀正	がしょう	Happy New Year
	祝賀	しゅくが	celebration

195 状	condition; letter ジョウ	丶	ン	⺦	⺦	状	状	状

Slender ⺦ and a dog 犬 combined, 状 first meant the appearance of a dog, and now it means appearance or condition in general.	現状	げんじょう	present situation
	礼状	れいじょう	letter of thanks
		… ◇ …	
	白状	はくじょう	confession

196 広	broad, wide; spread ひろ・い	丶	亠	广	広	広		

Roof 广 and arm ム combined, 広 means the space in the house where one can stretch one's arms widely. Thus 広 means wide.	広い	ひろい	spacious, wide
	広島	ひろしま	Hiroshima (place name)
	広場	ひろば	public square
		… ◇ …	

197 島	island しま、トウ	ノ	亻	冖	戸	自	自	鳥	鳥
		島	島						

鳥 represents 鳥 which is the pictograph of a bird. Combined with mountain 山, 島 means island with a mountain where flocks of birds alight for nesting.	島	しま	island
	半島	はんとう	peninsula
	島国	しまぐに	island country
		… ◇ …	
	無人島	むじんとう	uninhabited island

198 県　prefecture　ケン

1	冂	月	月	目	追	皁	県
県							

A prefecture 県 is a smaller 小 unit 目 of region.

県	けん	prefecture
広島県	ひろしまけん	Hiroshima-ken (prefecture name)
県立病院	けんりつびょういん	prefectural hospital
	… ◇ …	
県知事	けんちじ	governor

199 結　conclude; tie, bind　ケツ、(ケッ)

く	幺	玄	糸	糸	糸	糸	糸
糸	結	結	結				

吉 is the pictograph of a pot tightly covered with a lid. Combined with thread 糸, 結 means that a pot is covered and tied with a cord. Thus 結 means to tie, to bind, to conclude, or to end.

結果	けっか	result
結局	けっきょく	after all
	… ◇ …	
結成する	けっせいする	to organize
結語	けつご	concluding remarks
終結	しゅうけつ	conclusion

200 婚　marriage　コン

く	夂	女	女	妒	妒	妖	妖
婚	婚	婚					

The day 日 to become Mr. 氏 and Mrs. 女 is a wedding day.

結婚	けっこん	marriage
結婚式	けっこんしき	wedding ceremony
	… ◇ …	
婚約	こんやく	engagement
新婚旅行	しんこんりょこう	honeymoon

201 招	invite ショウ	一	寸	扌	扫	扪	护	招	招

召, a combination of sword 刀 and people 口, means the induction of men by a king using swords. 召 used as part of a kanji means to collect or call. Combined with hand 扌, 招 means to invite (or summon) someone (by waving a hand).

招待する	しょうたいする	to invite
招待状	しょうたいじょう	invitation card
	… ◇ …	
招集する	しょうしゅうする	to summon

202 返	return かえ・す、ヘン	一	厂	反	反	﹅反	汲	返	

Road 辶 and curved 反 combined, 返 means to return.

返す	かえす	to return
返事する	へんじする	to reply
	… ◇ …	
返品する	へんぴんする	to return goods

203 信	faith, trust, belief シン	ノ	イ	イ	伫	信	信	信	信
		信							

A man イ accepts the word 言 of others. Thus 信 means to believe.

返信	へんしん	reply
信じる	しんじる	to believe
信用	しんよう	trust
	… ◇ …	
信号	しんごう	signal
自信	じしん	self-confidence
通信	つうしん	communication

204 御	control; honorific prefix おん、ゴ、ギョ	ノ	ク	イ	彳	休	徃	御	徃
		徃	徔	御	御				

To go 彳 and to stop 止 together means to control. Pestle 午 and man 卩 together means to make hard things soft and smooth by pounding them. 御 was added as a prefix to the emperor's title to show respect.

御出席	ごしゅっせき	your (honorable) attendance
御中	おんちゅう	Dear Sirs
御主人	ごしゅじん	husband
	… ◇ …	
制御	せいぎょ	control
御礼	おんれい	thanks
御所	ごしょ	imperial palace

205 欠	lack, absence ケツ、（ケッ）	ノ	勹	ケ	欠				

This is the figure of a mouth wide open.

欠席	けっせき	absence
	… ◇ …	
出欠	しゅっけつ	attendance/absence
欠員	けついん	vacant position

206 配	distribute くば・る、ハイ、（パイ）	一	厂	帀	丙	西	酉	酉	酉
		酉	配						

酉 depicts a wine jar and 己 is a kneeling man. 配 shows a man kneeling by a wine jar, suggesting to allot, to distribute, or to pass out the jar's contents.

配る	くばる	to distribute
心配	しんぱい	worry
	… ◇ …	
支配する	しはいする	to control

207 達	reach; animate plural suffix タツ	一	十	土	士	寺	去	幸	幸
		幸	`幸	達	達				

Land 土, sheep or something good 羊, and come 辶, all combine to suggest that something good (like a sheep) will be delivered to you.	配達 速達 発達する	はいたつ そくたつ … ◇ … はったつする	delivery express mail to grow, to progress

208 求	want; request もと・める、キュウ	一	寸	寸	才	求	求	求	

I want to bring the water 水 level 一 to this point 、.	請求する 請求書 求める 求人 求職	せいきゅうする せいきゅうしょ … ◇ … もとめる きゅうじん きゅうしょく	to claim bill to request job offer job hunting

209 窓	window まど、ソウ	`	`	宀	宀	灾	空	突	突
		窓	窓	窓					

| 穴 means a hole. Big holes in a house are windows.

窓 窓口 同窓会 窓側の席 同窓生	まど まどぐち どうそうかい … ◇ … まどがわのせき どうそうせい	window window alumni association window seat alumnus

4 PRACTICE

Ⅰ. Write the readings of the following kanji in hiragana.

1. 年 賀 状   2. 請 求 書   3. 広 島 県   4. 結 婚 式

5. 招 待 する   6. 御 欠 席   7. 配 達   8. 窓 口

9. 返 信

10. 日本は、1道、1都、2府、43県に分かれています。

11. 天気がよい日は、窓を開けましょう。

12. フィリッピンも、日本も、島国です。

13. 県立病院で、はたらいています。

14. 心配しないでください。

15. 図書館の本を返します。

Ⅱ. Fill in the blanks with appropriate kanji.

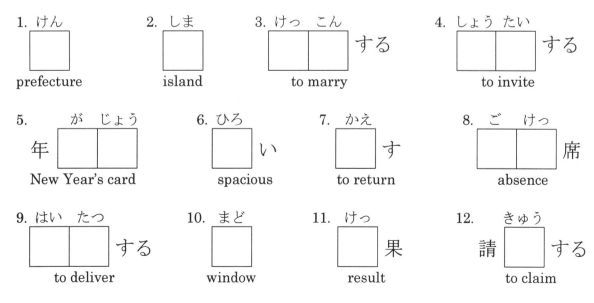

1. けん
□
prefecture

2. しま
□
island

3. けっ こん
□ □ する
to marry

4. しょう たい
□ □ する
to invite

5.
年 が じょう
□ □
New Year's card

6. ひろ
□ い
spacious

7. かえ
□ す
to return

8. ご けっ
□ □ 席
absence

9. はい たつ
□ □ する
to deliver

10. まど
□
window

11. けっ
□ 果
result

12. きゅう
請 □ する
to claim

Vending Machines　自動販売機

自動販売機	vending machine
氷 無し	without ice
砂糖	sugar
クリーム	cream
増量	more
減量	less
紙コップ専用	paper cup only
押す	push

デパートで買い物します

Shopping at a Department Store

DEPARTMENT STORES have existed in Japan since 1673. There are many chains now and they have many branches all over Japan and around the world. Japanese department stores specialize in clothing and household goods and have a wide range of stock. They have fancy, expensive, high-quality goods, and imported goods, too. You may request the department store to deliver an item to your home or to the home of someone else, if it is a gift, for which you may have to pay a certain amount. In the department stores, big signs direct you to floors with specific merchandise. Store clerks, some of whom speak English, may assist you, but it is always helpful to know some kanji at the department store.

1 INTRODUCTORY QUIZ

Look at the store directory below and refer to the words in VOCABULARY. Then try the following quiz.

Ⅰ. Mary went to a department store. On which floor will she find the goods she wants to buy? Refer to the information below.

1. 人形を買いたいです。＿＿＿＿＿＿階に行けばいいです。

2. 子供服は、＿＿＿＿＿＿階にあります。

3. 婦人服は、＿＿＿＿＿＿階にあります。

4. 催し物売場、＿＿＿＿＿＿階では、決算セールをしています。

5. 総合案内は、＿＿＿＿＿＿階にあります。ここでは、分からないことが聞けます。

6. 化粧品は、＿＿＿＿＿＿階にあります。

屋上		日本庭園　●ペットコーナー	
8	催場 美術展	●催し物売場 ●美術サロン	大食堂
7	総合案内 美術・リビング	●家具　●家庭用品　●和洋食器　●キッチン用品 ●絵画　●時計　●ベッド　●電気製品	化粧室
6	本・文具・おもちゃ スポーツ用品	●学用品　●絵本 ●人形　●プラモデル	化粧室
5	ベビー用品・子供用品 きもの	●子供服　●ベビー服　●ベビー用食器 ●各種着物　●和装小物　●ぞうり	
4	メンズ	●紳士服　●紳士コート　●ワイシャツ ●紳士肌着　●くつ下	
3	ヤング	●婦人服　●婦人洋品　●カジュアルスーツ ●ジーンズ　●スカーフ	軽食・喫茶
2	レディス	●婦人服　●ブラウス　●セーター　●婦人肌着 ●コート　●スカート	化粧室
1	ファッショングッズ	●化粧品　●ネクタイ　●スカーフ　●バッグ ●紳士・婦人くつ　●アクセサリー	
B1	食料品 地下鉄連絡口	●食料品　●野菜　●フルーツ　●茶　●コーヒー ●肉　●魚　●肉加工品　●和洋酒	化粧室
B2	駐車場		

本　館　の　ご　案　内

決算
総売りつくし
SALE

8階催場
EXHIBITION HALL

階　段

Note: Usually the *tenjikai, bijutsuten,* and *moyooshijo* or *saijo* and even a theater are on the top floor. Foreigners can buy goods duty-free.

2 VOCABULARY

Study the readings and meanings of these words to help you understand the INTRODUC-TORY QUIZ.

1.	本館	ほん かん	main building
2.	屋上	おく じょう	roof
3.	催場	さい じょう	bargain floor
4.	催し物売場	もよおし もの うり ば	bargain floor
5.	決算セール	けっ さん セール	sale, bargains
6.	美術展	び じゅつ てん	art gallery
7.	総合案内	そう ごう あん ない	customer service
8.	家具	か ぐ	furniture
9.	家庭用品	か てい よう ひん	household articles
10.	食器	しょっ き	tableware
11.	人形	にん ぎょう	dolls
12.	子供用品	こ ども よう ひん	children's goods
13.	子供服	こ ども ふく	children's wear
14.	紳士服	しん し ふく	men's wear
15.	婦人服	ふ じん ふく	women's wear
16.	化粧品	け しょう ひん	cosmetics
17.	食料品	しょく りょう ひん	food
18.	地下鉄連絡口	ち か てつ れん らく ぐち	exit for subway
19.	駐車場	ちゅう しゃ じょう	parking lot
20.	階段	かい だん	stairway

3 NEW CHARACTERS

Ten characters are introduced in this lesson. Use the explanations to help you understand and remember the characters. Study the compound words to increase your vocabulary.

形 供 服 催 決 算 総 化 粧 段

210 形

form, shape

かたち、ケイ、ギョウ

一　二　チ　开　开ノ　形ノ　形

A square frame 开 and decoration 彡 combined, 形 means shape.

形	かたち	shape
人形	にんぎょう	doll
円形	えんけい	circle
	… ◇ …	
形式	けいしき	form
図形	ずけい	figure
長方形	ちょうほうけい	rectangle
正方形	せいほうけい	square

211 供

attendant; offer

とも、（ども）、キョウ

ノ　イ　イ一　イ十　イ艹　イ艹　イ艹　供

A person イ is holding something with two hands 共. Thus 供 means to offer.

子供	こども	child
	… ◇ …	
お供する	おともする	to accompany
自供	じきょう	confession

212 服

clothes; obey

フク

丿　刀　月　月　月コ　肌コ　服　服

A man is kneeling 又 to his standing master 卩 to show obedience. Clothes 服 obey the body 月.

子供服	こどもふく	children's clothes
	… ◇ …	
婦人服	ふじんふく	women's wear
紳士服	しんしふく	men's wear
和服	わふく	Japanese clothing
洋服	ようふく	Western clothing
衣服	いふく	clothing

213 催

sponsor

もよお・す、サイ

ノ イ イ´ 仁 仙 仲 仲 仲
仲 併 併 催 催

An event attracts many people イ like a mountain 山 of birds 隹.

催場	さいじょう	bargain floor
催し物売り場	もよおしものうりば	bargain floor
主催	しゅさい	sponsorship
… ◇ …		
開催する	かいさいする	to hold (a meeting)

214 決

decide

き・める、ケツ、（ケッ）

ヽ ニ シ シフ 沪 決

This is a combination of water 氵, ユ, and person 人.

決める	きめる	to decide
… ◇ …		
決心する	けっしんする	to determine
決定する	けっていする	to decide
決意する	けついする	to determine

215 算

calculate

サン、（ザン）

ノ ヒ ケ ケ´ ケ ケケ ケケ 竹
竹 笘 笘 筲 算 算

Counting bamboo 竹 sticks with the eyes 目 and two hands 廾 means to calculate.

決算	けっさん	settlement of accounts
計算する	けいさんする	to calculate
予算	よさん	budget
… ◇ …		
引き算	ひきざん	subtraction
算数	さんすう	arithmetic
割り算	わりざん	division

216 総	general, overall ソウ	く	幺	幺	糸	弁	糸	糸'	糸ヽ
		糸厶	糸公	糸公	総	総	総		

Thread 糸 binds the public 公 and their heart 心 into one. Thus 総 means overall.

総合	そうごう	comprehensive
総会	そうかい	general meeting
	… ◇ …	
総理	そうり	prime minister
総数	そうすう	total number

217 化	change, transform カ、ケ	ノ	イ	イ'	イ'	化			

A young man イ changed into an old man with his head bending low ヒ, thus 化 means change.

文化	ぶんか	culture
国際化	こくさいか	internationalization
化学	かがく	chemistry
	… ◇ …	
変化する	へんかする	to change
消化する	しょうかする	to digest
化石	かせき	fossil

218 粧	adorn, make up ショウ	丶	ヽ'	ソ	半	米	米	米'	米ヽ
		米广	米广	粁	粧				

Ladies make up with pressed 庄 powder 米.

化粧品	けしょうひん	cosmetics
化粧室	けしょうしつ	ladies' room
	… ◇ …	

219 段	step, stairs ダン	ノ	イ	イ	ŕ	彳	自	虸	段
		段							

Steps 阝 and weapons 殳 lead up the steps to the throne.

階段	かいだん	staircase
	… ◇ …	
石段	いしだん	stone stairway
手段	しゅだん	means

4 PRACTICE

Ⅰ. Write the readings of the following kanji in hiragana.

1. 人 形　　　　2. 子 供　　　　3. 洋 服　　　　4. 催 場

5. 決 算　　　　6. 総 合　　　　7. 化 粧 品　　　8. 階 段

9. 化学の実験をするかどうか、決めていません。

10. 大きさや形によって、ちがいます。

11. 父は、空手の三段です。

12. 日本の文化について、調べます。

Ⅱ. Fill in the blanks with appropriate kanji.

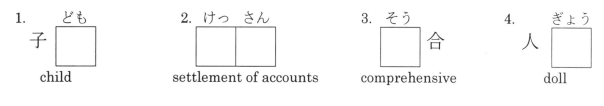

1. ども
子 □
child

2. けっ さん
□ □
settlement of accounts

3. そう
□ 合
comprehensive

4. ぎょう
人 □
doll

5. ふく
☐
clothes

6. さい
☐場
bargain floor

7. け しょう
☐☐品
cosmetics

8. だん
階☐
staircase

9. か
☐学
chemistry

10. き
☐める
to decide

5 SUPPLEMENT

Make words like the sample below using the kanji in the boxes.

子	供	学	食
洋	用	服	料
品	庭	人	粧
家	形	化	婦

1. <u>　化　粧　品　　　　　</u>

2. <u>　　　　　　　　　　　</u>

3. <u>　　　　　　　　　　　</u>

4. <u>　　　　　　　　　　　</u>

5. <u>　　　　　　　　　　　</u>

6. <u>　　　　　　　　　　　</u>

食料品

家庭用品

めいしを交換します

Exchanging Name Cards

WHEN YOU meet new people in Japan, it is common to exchange name cards, on which the person's name and business information are printed.   To read the name card, it is helpful to know some of the common kanji for personal names.   It is also useful to know kanji related to a person's position within a company. In this lesson, you will learn some Japanese surnames and also some terminology related to job titles at Japanese companies or other organizations and to home addresses.

1 INTRODUCTORY QUIZ

Look at the illustration below and refer to the words in VOCABULARY. Then try the following quiz.

Below are sample name cards.

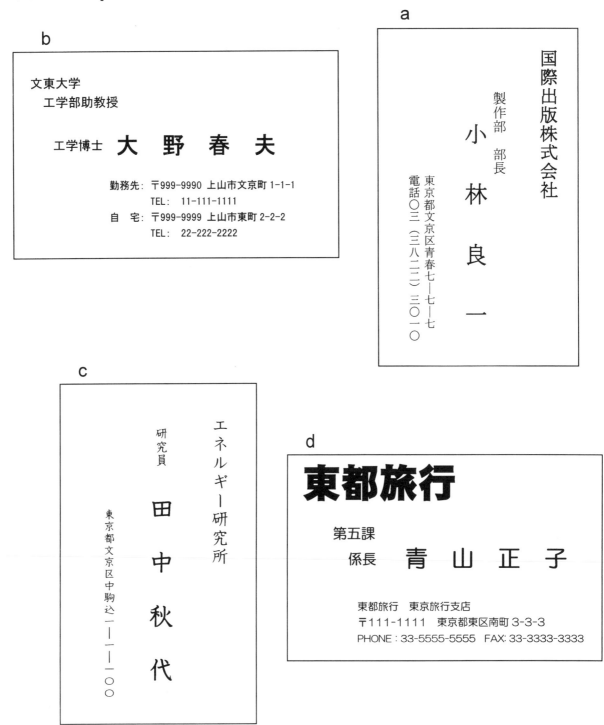

a

国際出版株式会社

製作部　部長

小　林　良　一

東京都文京区青春七一七一七
電話〇三（三八二二）三〇一〇

b

文東大学
　工学部助教授

工学博士　大　野　春　夫

勤務先：〒999-9990 上山市文京町 1-1-1
　　　　TEL：　11-111-1111
自　宅：〒999-9999 上山市東町 2-2-2
　　　　TEL：　22-222-2222

c

エネルギー研究所

研究員

田　中　秋　代

東京都文京区中駒込一一一一〇〇

d

東都旅行

第五課
係長　青　山　正　子

東都旅行　東京旅行支店
〒111-1111　東京都東区南町 3-3-3
PHONE：33-5555-5555　FAX：33-3333-3333

There are four name cards on the previous page. Which is whose name card?

Fill in the spaces with the correct letters (a～d) of the name cards.

1. (　　)

わたしは、旅行会
社につとめていま
す。1月にはハワイ
ツアーに出かける
予定です。

2. (　　)

わたしは、出版社
の製作部長です。
英語の本を作って
います。

3. (　　)

わたしは、研究員
です。毎日実験ば
かりしています。

4. (　　)

わたしは、大学の
助教授です。専門
は、コンピュータ
です。

2　VOCABULARY

Study the readings and meanings of these words to help you understand the INTRODUCTORY QUIZ.

1.	名刺	めい し	name card
2.	東都旅行	とう と りょ こう	Toto Travel Agent
3.	第五課	だい ご か	the fifth section
4.	係長	かかり ちょう	chief
5.	青山正子	あお やま まさ こ	Aoyama, Masako
6.	出版株式会社	しゅっ ぱん かぶ しき がい しゃ	publishing company
7.	製作部	せい さく ぶ	production department
8.	部長	ぶ ちょう	general manager
9.	小林良一	こ ばやし りょう いち	Kobayashi, Ryoichi
10.	エネルギー研究所	エネルギー けん きゅう しょ	Energy Research Institute
11.	研究員	けん きゅう いん	researcher
12.	田中秋代	た なか あき よ	Tanaka, Akiyo
13.	助教授	じょ きょう じゅ	associate professor
14.	大野春夫	おお の はる お	Ono, Haruo
15.	勤務先	きん む さき	place of work
16.	自宅	じ たく	home, residence
17.	旅行会社	りょ こう がい しゃ	travel agent
18.	実験	じっ けん	experiment

189

3 NEW CHARACTERS

Thirteen characters are introduced in this lesson. Use the explanations to help you understand and remember the characters. Study the compound words to increase your vocabulary.

課 係 長 青 社 作 林 員 秋 春 夫 助 授

---

220 課 lesson; section
カ

｜ 丶 二 亖 三 亖 言 言 言 | 訂 訶 訶 評 評 課 課 |

The boss tells 言 someone to work to bear fruit 果. Thus 課 means to assign someone a task.

一課	いっか	lesson one
学生課	がくせいか	student affairs section
… ◇ …		
教務課	きょうむか	academic affairs section
研究課題	けんきゅうかだい	research subject

---

221 係 relate to; charge; clerk
かかり、（がかり）、ケイ

ノ イ イ 仟 仟 任 仔 係 | 係 |

Man イ and thread 糸 combined, 係 means that a person is tied to or connected with a duty. Thus 係 means concern, relate to, duty or a person in charge.

係り	かかり	(person in) charge
学生係	がくせいがかり	student affairs section
… ◇ …		
関係	かんけい	relationship
関係者	かんけいしゃ	the person concerned

---

222 長 long; chief
なが・い、チョウ

丨	厂	丆	ㅌ	툐	長	長	長

This is the pictograph of an old man with long hair.

長い	ながい	long
係長	かかりちょう	section chief
会長	かいちょう	chairman
社長	しゃちょう	president
… ◇ …		
長男	ちょうなん	oldest son
特長	とくちょう	strong point

---

223 青 blue, green; unripe
あお・い、セイ

一	十	声	主	丯	青	青	青

青 is a combination of green bud 生 and the moon 月, suggesting blue and green.

青い	あおい	blue
青信号	あおしんごう	green signal
青山	あおやま	Aoyama (place name, family name)
… ◇ …		
青年	せいねん	youth

---

224 社 shrine; company, firm
シャ

丶	㇀	礻	ネ	ネ	礻	社	

ネ is the same as 示, which is the pictograph of an altar. Thus ネ indicates god. ネ combined with soil 土 or earth, the source of many products, means a shrine.

会社	かいしゃ	company
本社	ほんしゃ	head office
社会	しゃかい	society
… ◇ …		
社会人	しゃかいじん	member of society
社会主義	しゃかいしゅぎ	socialism

225 作	make つく・る、（づく・り）、サク、（サッ）、サ	ノ	イ	イ	仵	作	作	作

Man イ and hacksaw (indicating to cut) 乍 combined, 作 means to cut and make things.	作る	つくる	to make
	製作部	せいさくぶ	production section
	作り方	つくりかた	how to make
	作文	さくぶん	composition, essay
	… ◇ …		
	作家	さっか	author
	手作り	てづくり	handmade
	作業時間	さぎょうじかん	working hour

226 林	woods はやし、（ばやし）、リン	一	十	才	木	木	村	材	林

Two trees signify wood.	林	はやし	woods
	小林	こばやし	Kobayashi (family name)
	… ◇ …		
	山林	さんりん	mountains and forests
	(山)林学	(さん)りんがく	forestry

227 員	member イン	ヽ	口	口	戸	目	目	目	冒
		員	員						

Official members always talk 口 of money 貝.	社員	しゃいん	employee of a company
	係員	かかりいん	staff member in charge
	研究員	けんきゅういん	research fellow
	会員	かいいん	member
	全員	ぜんいん	all members
	役員	やくいん	executive officer
	定員	ていいん	capacity (number of persons)
	公務員	こうむいん	public servant
	… ◇ …		

| 228 秋 | autumn, fall
あき、シュウ | ノ | ニ | 千 | 禾 | 禾 | 禾 | 禾 | 秋 |
| | | 秋 | | | | | | | |

秌 is grain. People harvest grain and dry it with sunshine and fire 火 to store it. Thus 秋 is harvest time, autumn. Another version is that the color of grain turns into the color of fire 火. Thus 秋 means autumn.

秋	あき	autumn
秋田県	あきたけん	Akita-ken (prefecture name)
	… ◇ …	
秋分の日	しゅうぶんのひ	Autumnal Equinox Day
初秋	しょしゅう	early autumn

| 229 春 | spring
はる、シュン | 一 | 二 | 三 | 声 | 夫 | 夫 | 春 | 春 |
| | | 春 | | | | | | | |

夫 depicts a plant that is about to grow and the sun 日 combined, thus spring 春 is a season when trees and plants grow.

春	はる	spring
春夫	はるお	Haruo (man's first name)
青春	せいしゅん	youth
新春	しんしゅん	the New Year
春休み	はるやすみ	spring vacation
	… ◇ …	
春分の日	しゅんぶんのひ	Vernal Equinox Day

| 230 夫 | husband
おっと、フ、フウ | 一 | 二 | 夫 | 夫 | | | | |
| | | | | | | | | | |

This is the pictograph of a big 大 tall man with a topknot 一 on his head. 夫 means an adult man.

夫	おっと	husband
田中夫人	たなかふじん	Mrs. Tanaka
夫婦	ふうふ	Mr. and Mrs.
	… ◇ …	

193

231 助	help, assist; rescue たす・ける、ジョ	丨	冂	月	月	且	助	助	

Power 力 and to pile up 且 together means a lot of power. A lot of power enables you to help, assist, or rescue.	助ける　　たすける　　　　　　to help 助手　　　じょしゅ　　　　　　assistant, research associate 　　　　　　　… ◇ … 助言する　じょげんする　　　　to advise 助け合う　たすけあう　　　　　to help each other

232 授	give, grant; teach ジュ	一	十	才	扌	扌	扌	扌	扌
		护	押	授					

To extend a hand 扌 to a receiver 受 means to give.	教授　　　きょうじゅ　　　　professor 助教授　　じょきょうじゅ　　associate professor 　　　　　　… ◇ …

4 PRACTICE

I. Write the readings of the following kanji in hiragana.

1. 係 長　　　2. 課 長　　　3. 製 作 部　　　4. 青 春　　　5. 会 社

6. 助 教 授　7. 研 究 員　8. 夫 婦　　　9. 林　　　10. 青 い

11. 春と秋は、旅行シーズンです。

12. 夫は、公務員です。

13. 助手を一人、募集しています。

14. 春分の日と秋分の日は、夜と昼の長さがおなじです。

15. 母は、台所で朝ごはんを作っています。

Ⅱ. Fill in the blanks with appropriate kanji.

1. しゃ
会 ☐
company

2. かかりちょう
☐ ☐
section chief

3. つく
☐ る
to make

4. あお
☐ い
blue

5. しゃ ちょう
☐ ☐
president

6. はやし
☐
woods

7. はる
☐
spring

8. あき
☐
autumn

9. たす
☐ ける
to help

10. おっと
☐
husband

11. なが
☐ い
long

12. じゅ
教 ☐
professor

13. いん
会 ☐
member

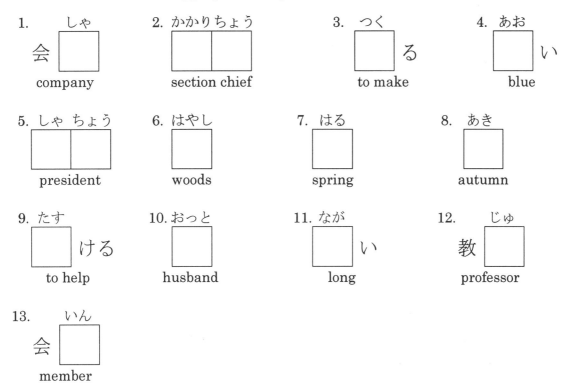

Job Titles

I. Here are many job titles having 長, which means head or chief.　How many of them do you know?

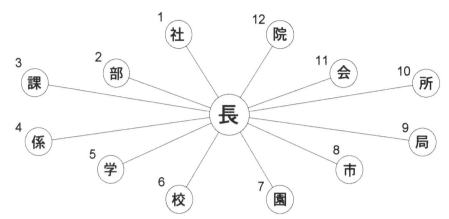

1.	会社	company	7.	保育園	day nursery
2.	営業部	sales department	8.	神戸市	Kobe city
3.	広報課	public relations section	9.	郵便局	post office
4.	経理係	accounting subsection	10.	研究所	research institute
5.	大学	university	11.	同窓会	alumni association
6.	学校	school	12.	病院	hospital

II. 員 means a member of an organization.　員 forms many job titles.

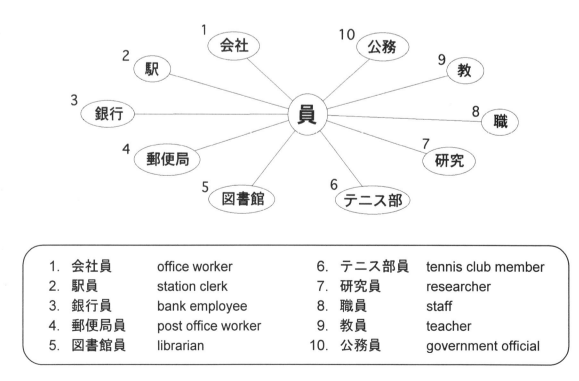

1.	会社員	office worker	6.	テニス部員	tennis club member
2.	駅員	station clerk	7.	研究員	researcher
3.	銀行員	bank employee	8.	職員	staff
4.	郵便局員	post office worker	9.	教員	teacher
5.	図書館員	librarian	10.	公務員	government official

休みの日はなにをしますか

What to Do on the Weekend

WHAT DO you do in your free time? There are many things you can enjoy: going to concerts, watching movies, attending art exhibitions at museums, playing sports, exercising at gyms, and having fun at amusement parks. In Japan, there are also seasonal activities. *Ohanami,* cherry blossom viewing, is a typical event in the spring, where people can enjoy eating and drinking under the cherry trees in their local park. Summer events include fireworks displays, and *bon-odori,* Japanese folk-dancing. Throughout the year, many festivals are held across Japan and are a major source of entertainment for the community.

1 INTRODUCTORY QUIZ

Look at the illustration below and refer to the words in VOCABULARY. Then try the following quiz.

I. The Smiths go to various places on weekends. Match the following tickets with the places. Write the correct letters (a～e) in the spaces provided.

1. 美術館 （　　　　）　　2. 遊園地 （　　　　）　　3. 音楽会 （　　　　）

4. 動物園 （　　　　）　　5. 博物館 （　　　　）

Ⅱ. Answer the following questions. Choose the correct answer.

1. おとながこの美術館に入る時、いくらですか。
（ a. 700 円　　b. 400 円 ）

2. この美術館は、いつでも入れますか。
（ a. はい　　b. いいえ ）

3. 臨時休館することがありますか。
（ a. はい　　b. いいえ ）

4. 20 人以上の団体は、安くなりますか。
（ a. はい　　b. いいえ ）

開館時間	午前10時から午後5時
	（入館は午後4時30分までにお願いします）

休 館 日	月曜日
	（ただし、祝日と重なる場合は、その翌日）
	年末年始（1週間）

※展示替えのため臨時休館することがあります。

入 館 料	一　般	700円
	大学・高校生	600円
	中・小学生	400円
	団体20名以上	各100円引

2　VOCABULARY

Study the readings and meanings of these words to help you understand the INTRODUCTORY QUIZ.

1. 美術館 （6）　び じゅつ かん　art museum
2. 音楽会 （12）　おん がく かい　concert
3. 映画館 （12）　えい が かん　movie theater
4. 遊園地 （8）　ゆう えん ち　amusement park
5. 開館時間　かい かん じ かん　opening hours
6. 休館日　きゅう かん び　closed day
7. 年末　ねん まつ　the end of the year
8. 年始　ねん し　the beginning of the year
9. 入館料　にゅう かん りょう　admission fee

10.	一般	いっ ぱん	the general public
11.	臨時休館	りん じ きゅう かん	temporarily closed
12.	団体²¹	だん たい	group

3 NEW CHARACTERS

Seven characters are introduced in this lesson.   Use the explanations to help you understand and remember the characters.   Study the compound words to increase your vocabulary.

術 楽 映 体 遊 般 臨

---

233 術 art; means
ジュツ

ノ ク オ 彳 彳 彳 彳 彳
彳 彳 術

朮, the pictograph of a plant with grain, suggests the fixed order as plants grow following the natural order.   To go 行 is combined, thus 術 means to do something following tradition.

美術館	びじゅつかん	art museum
	… ◇ …	
手術	しゅじゅつ	operation
学術	がくじゅつ	science

---

234 楽 music; enjoyable
たの・しい、ガク、ラク

ノ イ 白 白 白 泊 泊
泊 楽 楽 楽 楽

This is the pictograph of a tree with nuts on it.   The nuts make a delightful sound when they are shaken in a basket.   Thus 楽 means music, pleasure, easy, and comfortable.

楽しい	たのしい	enjoyable
音楽	おんがく	music
音楽会	おんがくかい	concert
	… ◇ …	
音楽家	おんがくか	musician
楽な	らくな	easy

235 映 reflect; project エイ

丨	冂	月	日	日丶	日丆	日巴	映
映							

Sunlight 日 directed at the center 央 of an object projects a figure on a screen behind the object.

映画	えいが	movie
映画館	えいがかん	movie theater
上映中	じょうえいちゅう	Now showing

… ◇ …

236 体 body からだ、タイ

ノ	イ	イ一	什	体	休	体	

A person's イ basic 本 part is the body 体.

団体	だんたい	group
体	からだ	body

… ◇ …

体重	たいじゅう	body weight
体力	たいりょく	physical strength
体育館	たいいくかん	gymnasium
気体	きたい	gaseous state

237 遊 play; be idle あそ・ぶ、ユウ

丶	亠	方	方	方丶	方	方	扩
斿	斿丶	游	遊				

Flag 斿 and child 子 combined, 斿 means to shake, to swing, or to swim. Road ⻌ is added and 遊 means to play, enjoy, or to be idle.

遊ぶ	あそぶ	to play
遊園地	ゆうえんち	amusement park

… ◇ …

遊歩道	ゆうほどう	promenade
周遊券	しゅうゆうけん	excursion ticket

238 般	general; carry ハン、（パン）	ノ	イ	力	行	自	舟	舟′	舟ˊ
		船	般						

Boat 舟 and action 殳 implies that a boat carries general items.	一般	いっぱん	general
		… ◇ …	
	一般化	いっぱんか	generalization
	全般	ぜんぱん	the whole

239 臨	confront リン	l	厂	厂	戶	戶	戶	臣	臣′
		臣ˊ	臣ˊ	臨	臨	臨	臨		

臣, a simplified figure of an eye, combined with things 品 and man イ, 臨 means that a man is glancing at various things. Thus 臨 means to confront.	臨時	りんじ	provisional
		… ◇ …	
	臨床	りんしょう	clinical
	臨終	りんじゅう	deathbed
	臨席	りんせき	presence
	臨海	りんかい	coastal, waterfront

4 PRACTICE

I. Write the readings of the following kanji in hiragana.

1. 美 術 館　　2. 音 楽　　　3. 映 画 館　　4. 遊 園 地

5. 一 般　　　6. 団 体　　　7. 臨 時

8. 二泊三日の旅行は、楽しかったです。

9. 公園で、子供が二人、遊んでいます。

10. お酒の飲みすぎは、体にわるいです。

11. 夏休みの間は、臨時休業します。

12. 今、どんな映画が上映中ですか。

Ⅱ. Fill in the blanks with appropriate kanji.

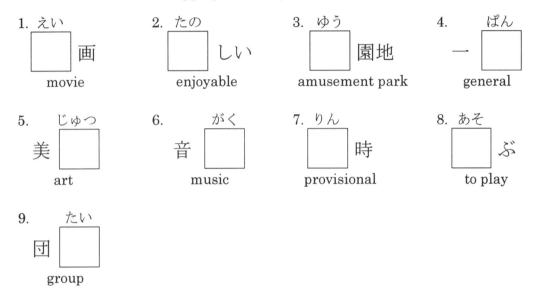

1. えい
□ 画
movie

2. たの
□ しい
enjoyable

3. ゆう
□ 園地
amusement park

4. ぱん
一 □
general

5. じゅつ
美 □
art

6. がく
音 □
music

7. りん
□ 時
provisional

8. あそ
□ ぶ
to play

9. たい
団 □
group

REVIEW EXERCISE   Lessons 16－21

Ⅰ. Many of the kanji you have learned in this textbook have common pronunciations. Shown below are compound words that include examples.

Write these kanji or corresponding letters in the blanks.

か

1. （　　）燃　burnable

2. （　　）長　section chief

3. 添（　　）物　additive

かん

4. 新（　　）線　bullet train

5. 変（　　）　conversion

6. （　　）字　kanji

せい

7. （　　）品　product

8. （　　）服　uniform

9. 音（　　）　voice

げん

10. （　　）気　fine

11. （　　）材料　raw material

12. 電（　　）　power

たい

13. 団（　　）　group

14. 渋（　　）　congestion

15. （　　）風　typhoon

てん

16. （　　）灯　lighting

17. （　　）気　weather

18. 自（　　）車　bicycle

こう

19. 学（　　）　school

20. 空（　　）　airport

21. 観（　　）　sightseeing

こう

22. 変（　　）　change

23. 有（　　）　valid

24. 良（　　）　good

---

a. 課   b. 可   c. 加   d. 漢   e. 幹   f. 換   g. 製   h. 声
i. 制   j. 源   k. 元   l. 原   m. 台   n. 滞   o. 体   p. 点
q. 天   r. 転   s. 光   t. 港   u. 校   v. 更   w. 好   x. 効

文化講座に申し込みます

Applying for a Culture Course

THE NOTICE boards in your local community display information distributed by the local government offices and are full of useful tips. Such information may pertain to free physical check-ups for residents, special lectures, performances, job openings for local government positions, or cultural course offerings. In this lesson, you will learn how to apply for a government-sponsored course.

1 INTRODUCTORY QUIZ

Look at the illustration below and refer to the words in VOCABULARY. Then try the following quiz.

講 座 名	期 間・時 間	定 員	参 加 費	そ の 他
初心者のための 生け花	5/10〜7/12(水)　（10回） 10:00〜11:30	10名	15,000 円	
お茶入門	5/9〜7/12(水)　（10回） 10:00〜11:30	10名	7,000 円	
日本語	5/12〜7/14(金)　（10回） 18:30〜20:00	10名	10,000 円 テキスト代を含む	
日本料理	5/11〜7/13(金)　（10回） 10:00〜12:00	15名	18,000 円	エプロンを持参 して下さい。

申し込み方法

●　往復はがきで申し込んで下さい。

●　定員に満たない場合は、中止することもあります。

●　締切日は、3月31日（金）当日消印有効

問い合わせ：　◇◇区役所、市民教育係　（045）000-0000

Please apply for the course you want to take.

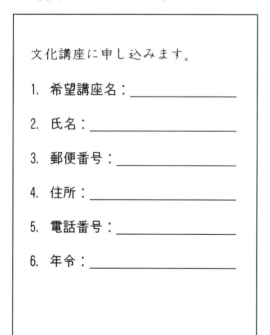

文化講座に申し込みます。

1. 希望講座名：＿＿＿＿＿＿＿

2. 氏名：＿＿＿＿＿＿＿＿＿

3. 郵便番号：＿＿＿＿＿＿＿

4. 住所：＿＿＿＿＿＿＿＿＿

5. 電話番号：＿＿＿＿＿＿＿

6. 年令：＿＿＿＿＿＿＿＿＿

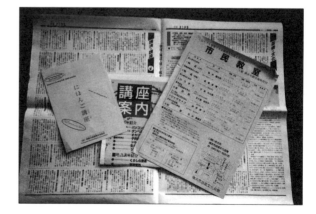

Note: International Divisions in city or ward offices and related international organizations offer various programs or services for foreigners.

2 VOCABULARY

Study the readings and meanings of these words to help you understand the INTRODUC-TORY QUIZ.

1.	講座名	こう ざ めい	name of a course
2.	定員[20]	てい いん	fixed number, capacity
3.	参加費[9]	さん か ひ	enrollment fee
4.	初心者	しょ しん しゃ	beginner
5.	生け花[6]	い け ばな	flower arrangement
6.	お茶入門	お ちゃ にゅう もん	introduction to tea ceremony
7.	初級	しょ きゅう	beginning class
8.	持参	じ さん	taking, bringing
9.	満たない	み たない	be short of
10.	締切日	しめ きり び	deadline
11.	当日[1]	とう じつ	day, the appointed day
12.	消印[13]	けし いん	postmark, cancellation mark
13.	有効	ゆう こう	valid, good
14.	問合わせ先[3]	とい あ わせ さき	a reference (to)
15.	希望講座	き ぼう こう ざ	a course one wants to take

3 NEW CHARACTERS

Eleven characters are introduced in this lesson. Use the explanations to help you understand and remember the characters. Study the compound words to increase your vocabulary.

座 参 初 心 持 締 効 満 問 希 望

240 座

seat; sit down

ザ

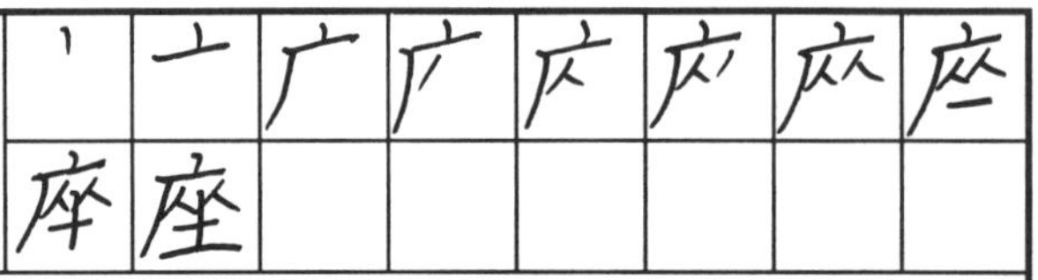

坐 is the pictograph of two persons 人人 sitting face to face on the ground 土 under a roof 广. Thus 座 means a place to sit.

講座	こうざ	course of lectures
座席	ざせき	seat
銀行の口座	ぎんこうのこうざ	bank account
銀座	ぎんざ	Ginza (place name)

… ◇ …

座長	ざちょう	chairman of a meeting
正座する	せいざする	to kneel upright, Japanese style

241 参

go; come; visit

サン

㕘 and 彡 both mean decoration. Thus 参 means to decorate oneself or dress up and attend a party or a ceremony.

参加する	さんかする	to take part in to attend
参加費	さんかひ	enrollment fee

… ◇ …

参議院	さんぎいん	House of Councilors
表参道	おもてさんどう	Omotesando (place name)

242 初

beginning, first

はじ・め、ショ

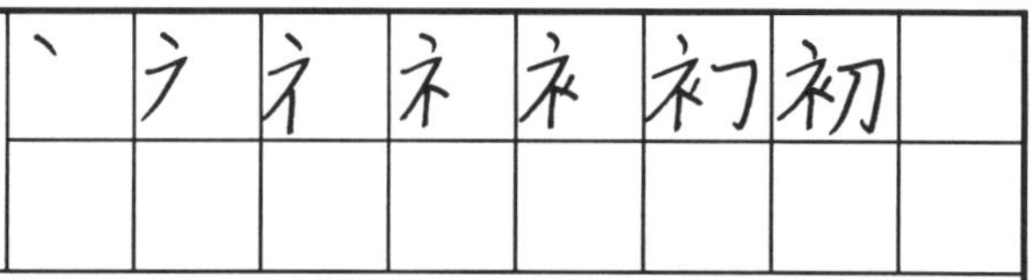

衤, the same as 衣, the pictograph of the kimono's V-shaped neckline means clothes. Imagine a tape-cutting ceremony celebrating the start of something. 衤 cloth and scissors 刀 are to start something.

初め	はじめ	the beginning
初めて	はじめて	for the first time
最初	さいしょ	first

… ◇ …

初級	しょきゅう	basic course
初日	しょにち	opening day

243 心	mind, heart; core こころ、シン	✓	忄	心	心			

This is the pictograph of a heart.

心	こころ	heart
初心者	しょしんしゃ	beginner
中心	ちゅうしん	center
心配する	しんぱいする	to worry
	… ◇ …	
心理学	しんりがく	psychology
重心	じゅうしん	center of gravity

244 持	have, possess, hold も・つ、ジ	一	十	才	扌	扩	拝	拝	持
		持							

寺, a combination of land or place 土 and rules 寸, means a temple, because a temple 寺 used to be the place to make rules. 寺 combined with hand, 持 means to hold or possess power, because temples possessed power and wealth.

持つ	もつ	to hold
持参する	じさんする	to bring with
持ち物	もちもの	possessions
気持ち	きもち	feeling
	… ◇ …	
金持ち	かねもち	rich people
支持する	しじする	to support
所持品	しょじひん	belongings

245 締	tie, tighten し・める	く	乡	幺	牟	糸	糸	糸	糸
		紵	紵	紵	絆	絆	締	締	

帝 is the pictograph of a torch made of many sticks which are bound into one. Thus 帝 alone means emperor who unites the nation into one. Rope 糸 and together 帝 means to bind, to tie, or to close.

締める	しめる	to tie
締切日	しめきりび	deadline date
	… ◇ …	

246 効	effective コウ	`丶`	`亠`	`广`	`六`	`亥`	`交`	`䒑`	`効`

Mix 交 and power 力 means effect, because things go smoothly (effectively) and well by mixing power.

有効	ゆうこう	valid
無効	むこう	invalid
	… ◇ …	
有効期限	ゆうこうきげん	validity period
効力	こうりょく	effect; validity

247 満	full; fulfill み・ちる、マン	`丶`	`冫`	`氵`	`氵-`	`汁`	`汁`	`洪`	`洪`
		`洪`	`満`	`満`	`満`				

The vase is filled 満 both 両 with water 氵 and flowers (plants).

満ちる	みちる	to be full
	… ◇ …	
満席	まんせき	No seats available
満員	まんいん	full capacity
満開	まんかい	full-bloom
不満な	ふまんな	dissatisfied
満月	まんげつ	full moon

248 問	question, problem と・う、モン	`l`	`冂`	`厂`	`尸`	`厃`	`門`	`門`	`門`
		`門`	`問`	`問`					

Mouth 口 and gate 門 combined, 問 means to ask, because people can't see what is behind the closed gate and ask about it.

問い	とい	question
問い合わせる	といあわせる	to inquire
質問	しつもん	question
	… ◇ …	
学問	がくもん	studies

249 希	hope, desire; rarity キ	ノ	メ	ㄨ	斉	齐	希	希

Cross ㄨ and 布 combined, 希 means a cloth tightly woven, through which it is difficult to see things. Thus 希 means hope.

希望する　きぼうする　to hope
… ◇ …

250 望	desire, wish, hope のぞ・む、ボウ	`	亠	亡	亡´	亡ク	亡タ	亡タ	亡ク
		亡ク	亡ク	望					

The king 王 is looking forward to seeing the moon 月 which has not appeared 亡. Thus 望 means to look forward.

希望者　きぼうしゃ　applicant
有望な　ゆうぼうな　promising
… ◇ …
望む　のぞむ　to hope
要望する　ようぼうする　to demand

4 PRACTICE

Ⅰ. Write the readings of the following kanji in hiragana.

1. 講 座　　2. 参 加 費　　3. 初 心 者

4. 持 参 する　　5. 有 効　　6. 問 い 合 わ せ る

7. 希 望　　8. 満 ち る　　9. 締 切 日

10. 外国へ旅行するのは、初めてです。

11. パソコンの使い方について、質問があります。

12. 文化講座に参加する人は、エプロンを持ってきてください。

13. 人の心の中は、よく分かりません。

II. Fill in the blanks with appropriate kanji.

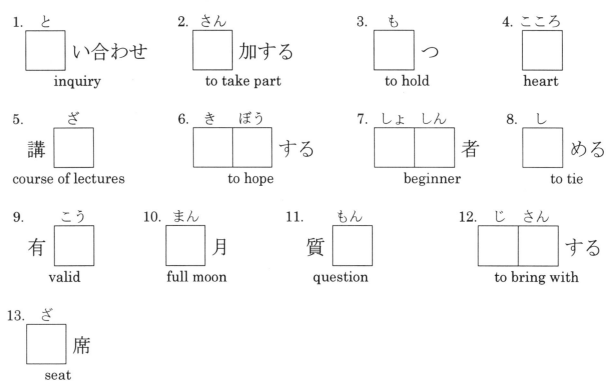

1. と
[   ]い合わせ
inquiry

2. さん
[   ]加する
to take part

3. も
[   ]つ
to hold

4. こころ
[   ]
heart

5. ざ
講[   ]
course of lectures

6. き ぼう
[|]する
to hope

7. しょ しん
[|]者
beginner

8. し
[   ]める
to tie

9. こう
有[   ]
valid

10. まん
[   ]月
full moon

11. もん
質[   ]
question

12. じ さん
[|]する
to bring with

13. ざ
[   ]席
seat

Appendix A

The Main Radicals Presented in This Book and Some Examples

I. へん (left part) ▐

1.	シ	water	活、港、酒、添、温、源、油、泊、海、浴、決、満、漢、渋、滞
2.	イ	man	価、供、側、低、化、係、体、優、信、作、催
3.	糸	thread	続、組、綿、締、編、結、総
4.	木	tree	校、枚、村、植、材、林、検
5.	彳	step	待、得、役、復、御
6.	言	speech	説、請、調、設、課
7.	扌	hand	招、授、持、換、指
8.	車	vehicle	軽、転、輪
9.	女	woman	婦、好、婚
10.	冫	ice	冷、凍

II. つくり (right part) ▐

1.	刂	sword, knife	利、到、制、剤、別、刷、削、初
2.	殳	lance shaft	役、設、殿、段、般

III. かんむり (top part) ▬

1.	艹	plant	花、荷、蔵、菜、英、落
2.	宀	roof	家、宅、客、容、宿、字

IV. あし (bottom part) ▬

1.	貝	money	賃、賀、質

V. かまえ (enclosing part) ▯

1.	門	gate	問、関
2.	囗	enclosure	園

VI. にょう (left and bottom part) ◣

1.	辶	move ahead	送、運、選、返、達、遊

VII. たれ (top and left part) ◤

1.	广	slanting roof	庭、度、広、座
2.	厂	cliff	原、圧

Appendix B
Kanji Compounds in This Book

Ⅰ. Main Types of Compounds and Some Examples

Type 1.　Adjectives ＋ Noun:

外交、石庭、自宅、公園、関税、原価、塩水、社宅、家族、果物、金額、校長、新春、初夏、現代、台所、婚約、島国、役人、旅費、母校、両方、大浴場、関東、定価、好物、内職

Type 2.　Verb (Modifier) ＋ Noun:

旅客、冷房、洗剤、圧力、講座、植木、願書、製法、集収日、希望者

Type 3.　Adverb ＋ Verb:

自転、予報、公認、要望、公示、再会、正座、速報

Type 4.　Verb ＋ Noun (Objective):

出席、欠員、観光、返信、設備、転校、求人、送風、発音、作文、禁酒、制度、指名、賞味、開催、録画、加工、分類、受賞、欠席、決心、休職

Type 5.　Pair of Synonyms:

良好、会合、記録、職業、教育、容器、回復、配達、参加、関係、変更、主要、存在、添加、建設、発育、招集、終了、支持、消化、結成、快晴、収入、変化、階段、修了、発行、宿泊

Type 6.　Pair of Antonyms:

往復、父母、出欠、朝夕、強弱、新古、公私、天地、高低、夫婦、晴雨

Ⅱ. Kanji Used in Many Compounds and Some Examples

力：　電力、水力、風力、火力、全力、重力、動力、自力、有力、無力、人力、力士
家：　家賃、家主、家内、家庭、大家、専門家、作家、画家、音楽家
風：　和風、洋風、強風、弱風、冷風、温風、台風、校風、社風、家風、古風
公：　公団、公園、公示、公平、不公平、公立、公式
共：　共通、共益、共学、共和国、公共
交：　交通、交番、交流、交際、外交、国交
役：　役所、市役所、区役所、役人、主役、役目
価：　特価、定価、物価、原価、安価、高価
直：　直通、直線、直接、直前、直後、直行、直売、直送

税： 税金、免税、免税店、税関、無税、国税、消費税

変： 変更、変化、不変、大変、変換

送： 送信、送料、運送、郵送、直送、送別会

合： 会合、合計、合流, 組合、待合室

真： 写真、真上、真空、真理、真実

職： 職業、職員、無職、休職、内職、現職

集： 収集、集積、募集、集金、特集、集中、作文集、集会、集合

積： 集積、集積回路、体積、面積、容積

軽： 軽食、軽工業、軽音楽、軽油、軽量、軽快

重： 重工業、重量、重油、重要、重力、重体、体重

制： 制度、税制、学制、強制、申込制

以： 以外、以内、以上、以下、以後、以前

私： 私立、私費、公私、私用、私生活、私見

町： 町内、町長、町村、大手町、有楽町、町名

校： 校長、校内、校風、校正、学校、転校、母校

化： 電化、強化、国際化、文化、変化、分化、消化

再： 再生、再発行、再会、再利用、再入国

器： 容器、食器、消化器、消火器、楽器、受話器、器用

収： 収集、収入、月収、年収、回収、収容

園： 公園、動物園、植物園、入園、庭園、開園

Appendix C
Answers to the Quizzes

第一課　：　省略 (Omitted)

第二課　：　省略 (Omitted)

第三課　：　Ⅰ．1－c　　2－d　　3－b　　4－e　　5－f　　6－a
　　　　　　Ⅱ．1－a　　2－b　　3－c　　4－d　　5－e

第四課　：　省略 (Omitted)

第五課　：　省略 (Omitted)

第六課　：　1－a　　2－b　　3－k　　4－d　　5－e　　6－g
　　　　　　7－h　　8－f　　9－c　　10－i　　11－j

第七課　：　1－b　　2－c　　3－a　　4－b　　5－a　　6－b

第八課　：　c

第九課　：　1－a, c　　　　2－a, b, d　　3－b, d　　　　4－a

第十課　：　1－a　　2－c　　3－b　　4－b　　5－c　　6－d

第十一課：　1－h　　2－i　　3－a　　4－d　　5－f　　6－g　　　7－e

第十二課：　1－d　　2－c　　3－f　　4－a　　5－e　　6－g　　　7－h

第十三課：　1－d　　2－e　　3－h　　4－g　　5－c
　　　　　　6－b　　7－a　　8－i　　9－f　　10－j

第十四課：　1－a　　2－a　　3－a

第十五課：　Ⅰ．省略 (Omitted)

　　　　　　Ⅱ．1－a, c　　　2－b, d

第十六課：　1－j　　2－e　　3－c　　　4－k　　5－g (a)　6－i
　　　　　　7－a (g)　8－b　　9－f　　10－d　　11－h

第十七課：　Ⅰ．省略 (Omitted)

　　　　　　Ⅱ．1－c　　2－e　　3－d　　4－f　　5－a　　6－b

第十八課：　Ⅰ．省略 (Omitted)
　　　　　　Ⅱ．省略 (Omitted)

弟十九課：　1－6　　2－5　　3－2,3　　4－8　　5－7　　6－1

第二十課　　：　　1−d　　2−b　　　3−c　　　　4−a

第二十一課：　　Ⅰ．1−d　　2−a　　3−c　　　4−b　　　5−e

　　　　　　　　　Ⅱ．1−a　　2−b　　3−a　　　4−a

第二十二課：　　省略 (Omitted)

Answers to the Review Exercises

Lessons 1–9 : 　　Ⅰ．1〜5 (a, d, f, h, l)　　　6〜10 (b, g, k, n, p)　　　11〜13 (c, i, o)

　　　　　　　　14〜16 (e, j, m)

　　　　　　Ⅱ．1−m　　2−c　　3−f　　4−r　　5−d

　　　　　　　　6−e　　7−i　　8−s　　9−l　　10−t

　　　　　　　　11−j　　12−h　　13−g　　14−k　　15−b

Lessons 10–15 : 　Ⅰ．1−f　　2−b, i　　3−a　　4−g　　5−c　　6−e　　7−d, h

　　　　　　　Ⅱ．1−e, i, m　　2−b, h, k　　3−d, f, j　　4−a, g, n　　5−c, l, o

Lessons 16–21 : 　1−b　　2−a　　3−c　　4−e　　5−f　　6−d　　7−g

　　　　　　　　8−i　　9−h　　10−k　　11−l　　12−j　　13−o　　14−n

　　　　　　　　15−m　　16−p　　17−q　　18−r　　19−u　　20−t　　21−s

　　　　　　　　22−v　　23−x　　24−w

On-Kun Index

The words in this index are taken from the kanji charts. *On-yomi* in katakana and *kun-yomi* in hiragana are followed by the kanji, their lesson numbers, and page numbers. Hiragana after (・) indicates *okurigana*. Modified readings in (　) follow after original readings.

キョウ	供	19-182	コウ	効	22-210	シャ	社	20-191	
ギョウ	形	19-182	ゴウ	合	3-45	ジャク	弱	1-112	
			こえ	声	12-118	シュ	酒	6-70	
【く　ク】			（ごえ）	声	12-118	ジュ	授	20-194	
グ	具	6-69	こころ	心	22-209	シュウ	集	2-35	
くば・る	配	18-175	こめ	米	6-69	シュウ	収	7-76	
くみ	組	5-63	ころも	衣	10-102	シュウ	秋	20-193	
（ぐみ）	組	5-63	コン	婚	18-173	ジュウ	重	12-119	
くも・る	曇	17-162				ジュウ	渋	16-153	
くら	蔵	9-96	**【さ　サ】**			シュク	宿	14-136	
			ザ	座	22-208	（ジュク）	宿	14-136	
【け　ケ】			サイ	菜	10-105	ジュツ	術	21-200	
け	毛	10-104	サイ	再	12-119	シュン	春	20-193	
（げ）	毛	10-104	サイ	最	17-164	ショ	初	22-208	
ケ	化	19-184	サイ	催	19-183	ジョ	除	13-126	
ケイ	軽	6-71	ザイ	在	2-35	ジョ	徐	16-152	
ケイ	型	16-153	ザイ	材	9-92	ジョ	助	20-194	
ケイ	形	19-182	ザイ	剤	10-102	ショウ	賞	9-94	
ケイ	係	20-190	サク	削	13-126	ショウ	招	18-174	
けず・る	削	13-126	サク	作	20-192	ショウ	粧	19-184	
ケツ	結	18-173	（サッ）	作	20-192	ジョウ	状	18-172	
ケツ	欠	18-175	さけ	酒	6-70	ショク	職	4-54	
（ケッ）	欠	18-175	（さか）	酒	6-70	ショク	植	9-92	
ケツ	決	19-183	（ざか）	酒	6-70	しら・べる	調	9-93	
（ケッ）	決	19-183	サツ	刷	13-127	しるし	印	13-127	
ケン	建	1-25	（サッ）	刷	13-127	しろ・い	白	10-104	
ケン	検	13-128	サン	算	19-183	シン	身	2-36	
ケン	県	18-173	（ザン）	算	19-183	シン	真	6-68	
ゲン	元	2-36	サン	参	22-208	シン	信	18-174	
ゲン	現	8-87				シン	心	22-209	
ゲン	原	9-92	**【し　シ】**			ジン	神	15-145	
ゲン	限	9-94	シ	指	7-79				
ゲン	源	12-120	シ	私	8-83	**【す　ス】**			
			シ	脂	9-93	スウ	数	17-163	
【こ　コ】			ジ	示	8-86	（ズウ）	数	17-163	
コ	戸	1-25	ジ	次	12-118	す・き	好	1-27	
コ	古	6-70	ジ	寺	15-144				
ゴ	御	18-175	ジ	字	17-163	**【せ　セ】**			
コウ	交	1-26	ジ	持	22-209	セイ	請	4-53	
コウ	好	1-27	しお	塩	5-61	セイ	姓	4-54	
コウ	向	1-28	シツ	質	10-103	セイ	制	7-78	
コウ	公	2-34	しぶ	渋	16-153	セイ	製	9-95	
コウ	港	3-42	しま	島	18-172	セイ	声	12-118	
コウ	更	4-52	しめ・す	示	8-86	セイ	晴	17-161	
コウ	校	8-85	し・める	締	22-209	セイ	青	20-191	
コウ	光	15-144	シャ	写	6-68	ゼイ	税	3-44	

Vocabulary Index

The words in this index are taken from the vocabulary lists and kanji charts in lessons 1–22.